People and Reefs

Successes and Challenges in the Management of Coral Reef Marine Protected Areas

Regional Seas Reports and Studies No. 176

UNEP 2004

FOREWORD

Coral Reefs are among the world's richest and most spectacular ecosystems. Their contribution to marine biodiversity is enormous. While covering less than 1 per cent of the ocean floor, they support an estimated 25 per cent of all marine life. More than one billion people in the tropics benefit directly from coral reef resources for food and as a source of income through activities related to fishing and tourism.

As productive as coral reefs are, they are also among the most fragile ecosystems. The world's reefs have been suffering a dramatic decline in recent decades as tropical ecosystems begin to suffer the effects of human activities and global environmental change. Some 10 per cent of the world's reefs may already be degraded beyond recovery, and another 30 per cent are in decline.

Coral reefs were accorded a high priority for protection under Agenda 21 by the 1992 United Nations Conference on Environment and Development. The international community responded with several initiatives, among which was the International Coral Reef Initiative (ICRI), launched in 1994. Under ICRI's guidance, the International Coral Reef Action Network (ICRAN) was established in 2000. ICRAN is a global partnership dedicated to halting the trend of degradation of coral reefs and related ecosystems worldwide and maintaining their biodiversity, health and productivity .

ICRAN activities are implemented at the site and community level through four of the UNEP Regional Seas programmes. A number of these important coastal coral reef management initiatives were presented at the International Tropical Marine Ecosystem Management Symposium II (ITMEMS II), held in Manila, Philippines, in March 2003, featuring case studies from the Wider Caribbean, Eastern African, East Asian Seas and South Pacific regions. Although they encompass a variety of regional, social and economic contexts, the case studies highlight several important common issues: the importance of stakeholder involvement, empowerment and community support, capacity building and public awareness and education. These case studies also illustrate that, though geographic locations may differ, the challenges and threats which reefs and people face are the same.

"People and Reefs: successes and challenges in the management of coral reef marine protected areas" offers an opportunity to share the experiences and learn the lessons of the many communities and individuals who share responsibility for the sustainable management of these endlessly fascinating and bountiful ecosystems. Only by working together and sharing our knowledge can we hope to preserve coral reefs for the benefit of future generations.

– Klaus Töpfer, Executive Director,
United Nations Environment Programme

TABLE OF CONTENTS

CONTENTS

ACKNOWLEDGEMENTS

The editor, Colette Wabnitz, would like to thank first and foremost Alison Glass for her invaluable assistance in providing required documents and pictures, as well as for her comments, suggestions, and feedback throughout the editorial phase of this publication. Furthermore, the editor would like to extend thanks to Fernando Simal for providing additional necessary data on the Bonaire Marine Park study; Rebecca Mitchell for making pictures of Fiji available for use in this report; Lauretta Burke for allowing the reproduction of two tables from the Reefs at Risk study in Southeast Asia; and Danielle Smith for commenting on and adding detailed information to the Regional Seas programmes table. The editorial assistance of Robert Ahrens, Cecile Wabnitz, Chantal Wabnitz and Mike Mascia is also kindly acknowledged. Comments and suggestions provided by Ellik Adler, Hanneke van Lavieren, Nikki Meith, Agneta Nilsson, Mary Power, Jerker Tamelander and Kristian Teleki significantly improved this manuscript.

Financial support for the work of ICRAN which forms the content of this publication has been generously provided the UN Foundation, the Goldman Fund and UNEP.

EXECUTIVE SUMMARY

This report documents 13 coastal coral reef management initiatives, operated under the ICRAN framework. Although, all case studies were formally accepted, due to unforeseen circumstances/political tensions only eight of these initiatives were presented at the International Tropical Marine Ecosystem Management Symposium 2 (ITMEMS 2), held in Manila, Philippines, 24–27 March 2003, as part of the ICRAN-sponsored session, "The Role of Protected Areas in Management". In this workshop, in addition to presentations, UNEP Regional Seas, partners, managers and practitioners from a number of ICRAN sites shared their experiences in management of, lessons learned from, and challenges faced by their particular park. They also discussed how ICRAN can contribute towards addressing site priorities and needs as well as future learning opportunities.

Before describing these case studies, this report introduces some of the key issues in coral reef conservation and the role of ICRAN and the UNEP Regional Seas Programme. First, it gives a brief introduction to the natural resources and economic opportunities that coral reef ecosystems provide. The report then highlights marine protected areas (MPAs) as one of the most applicable, useful and comprehensive management strategies available to local communities and local, national and international institutions (e.g., government, academic, scientific, non-governmental and donor organizations) to mitigate the threats faced by reef ecosystems and foster sustainable use of marine and coastal resources worldwide. A description of ICRAN and UNEP's Regional Seas programmes follows, noting their geographic coverage, how these two institutions came about and developed, their *modus operandi*, and some of the priority issues being addressed by both.

This report includes seven case studies from the **Wider Caribbean Region.** The first one focuses on the capacity building opportunity provided by the UNEP-CEP training of trainers programme, while the second study looks at the community-based coastal resource management and marine biodiversity conservation experience in Sian Ka'an Biosphere Reserve, Mexico. The third project analyses rules and zoning issues in the management plan of Chinchorro Banc Biosphere Reserve, Mexico. The opportunities and challenges of using admission fees as a funding source at a small scale, tourism dependant MPA, Bonaire, are presented in the fourth study. The fifth example of reserve management, describes how – from MPA implementation to today – relationships have been strengthened to ensure effective management in the Soufriere Marine Management Area (SMMA). The sixth case study details the role of the honorary game wardens and fisheries inspectors of the Portland Bight Protected Area, Jamaica, in the context of community policing and the country's "culture of system-beating". The seventh study depicts the process of conflict resolution between inter-sectoral stakeholders in the Buccoo Reef Marine Park coastal zone, Tobago, using Pigeon Point as an example.

Two case studies are included for the **Eastern African Region.** The first case outlines the implementation of ICRAN activities at the Malindi/Watamu MPA. The second study examines the challenges and opportunities of managing marine reserves, focusing on the Dar es Salaam Marine Reserves System, Tanzania, a MPA surrounded by poor populations and close to a vast urban setting.

Two case studies are described in the context of the **East Asian Seas Region.** The first one focuses on the development of a conservation strategy for Gili Matra Marine Natural Recreation Park, West Nusa Tenggara Province, Indonesia, taking into account sources of conflicts and the park's potential value, as well as environmental socio-economic conditions of surrounding communities. The second case describes the co-management initiative in coastal resource management and marine biodiversity conservation experience in Bunaken National Marine Park, Indonesia.

Two case studies are presented from the **South Pacific Region.** The first project discusses the development of a multiple-use management plan by the island communities of Jaluit Atoll that would ensure marine and coastal conservation while allowing for sustainable use of biological resources. The second study describes hands-on coral transplantation and restocking experiments, chiefly in Fiji, and analyses the feasibility of such management techniques as a means to accelerate the recovery of coral reef habitats and fisheries resources in MPAs.

Although the case studies present a variety of issues, contexts and responses, and were implemented in four regions characterized by very diverse socio-economic and political situations, all sites highlighted common features:

- Threats to coral reefs – overfishing and associated declines in fish catches; use of destructive fishing practices; pollution (marine and land-based); increasing population pressure; as well as poor development and land use practices.

- Management challenges – resource use conflicts; unsustainable development; and lack of education and public awareness, adequate management of resources, enforcement, monitoring, financial stability and human capacity.

- Lessons learned – the need for: greater community empowerment and involvement; sustained and extensive consultation between stakeholders; proactive and innovative education and public awareness campaigns; improved communication and transparency between all involved members; strong management partnerships to secure long term financial stability; development of management plans based on ecological as well as socio-economic data and linked to regular monitoring programmes; implementation of clearly defined zoning regulations to reduce conflicts between stakeholders; and enhanced enforcement efforts.

PART I
INTRODUCTION

Coral reefs, often referred to as the rainforests of the sea, cover less than 1% of the marine environment, but are among the most diverse, complex, productive and beautiful ecosystems on Earth [1-3]. Beyond their remarkable biodiversity, reefs' benefits include the safeguarding of lives, cultures, and entire economies. They encourage the development of tourism; act as vital protection against storms and thus erosion [4]; provide 10% of tropical countries' fishing harvests as well as 25% of the fish catch of developing countries [1]; and are a source of employment and leisure [2]. Increasing pressure on these ecosystems has led to reef degradation and declines in associated biodiversity; is linked to the loss of economic opportunities; and is presenting growing challenges to the livelihoods of local communities. It is also associated with increasing poverty levels in most coral reef areas around the world, highlighting the crucial economic and social roles of coral reefs in the function and stability of many of the world's poorest coastal and island human communities. Humans need coral reefs; consequently, effective management that promotes sustainable use of marine resources is critical. One of the most widespread and advocated mechanisms for protecting coral reefs is the designation of Marine Protected Areas (MPAs) that implement (preferably large-scale) ecosystem-based management. No-take marine reserves provide particularly effective means of addressing coastal and marine biodiversity conservation [5] as well as fisheries issues, whilst also creating opportunities for sustainable use, alternative livelihoods, and stewardship.

In order to achieve success in Integrated Coastal Management (ICM), participatory planning and decision-making have been highlighted as critical elements of effective management and sustainable use of marine and coastal resources. A key element for successful community participation, information dissemination and education is to understand the local context, including the premise that community participation in management may work best in small, localized MPAs. Co-management – often the framework advocated for the effective management of reserves and the relationships upon which the system is built – need to be flexible. Thus, although the structure can and should involve a variety of stakeholders (i.e. private sector, academic, government, non-government, community-based organizations, and others), the interests of local subsistence resource users must be at the forefront. Furthermore, to ensure MPA objectives, effective enforcement of legal controls is essential, as without it, reserves and ICM programmes will not provide their intended benefits to the marine ecosystems and communities that depend upon them. Moreover, awareness of management activity, the responsibilities and rights of resource and MPA users, and the issues that management must address are essential.

There is also an urgent need for greater recognition by government, funding agencies, and Non-Governmental Organizations (NGOs), that effective enforcement of marine resource use regulations requires much greater financial and political support. Active engagement with the private sector is critical for long-term success in sustaining and conserving coral reefs and related ecosystems, whilst providing food and sustainable economic opportunities to local communities. Well-designed and targeted research, and scientific as well as socio-economic monitoring programmes, are essential components of tropical marine ecosystem management. Unfortunately, even given this knowledge, MPAs average a 10% success rate worldwide, indicating that the challenge of fulfilling both environmental conservation and human needs remains. Failure in effective management and enforcement of legislation in a number of marine parks to date have mainly been attributed to lack of: capacity, political will, buy-in by local stakeholders, consultation, lack of awareness about coral reef values and threats, as well as sustainable funds and the effective targeting of these.

The International Coral Reef Action Network (ICRAN) co-organized a session at the Second International Tropical Marine Ecosystems Management Symposium (ITMEMS 2) focusing on 'The Role of Protected Areas in Management.' At the session, the United Nations Environment Programme (UNEP) Regional Seas partners and site managers of ICRAN presented a number of papers and case studies on the sustainable management and conservation of coral reefs at ICRAN sites in the Caribbean Sea, Indian, and Pacific Oceans.

To date, these papers have not been published, nor finalized, but they contain a wealth of information, experiences, and lessons learned. As such, they constitute an opportunity to showcase one of the most successful aspects of the ICRAN partnership and the progress made by its UNEP Regional Seas partners.

To maximize the global benefit and reach of the papers, they have been edited into a UNEP Regional Seas Reports and Studies series. The studies are presented within a general framework, introducing ICRAN and the Regional Seas mandate and action arena, as well as placed within the environmental and socio-economic context and activities of the partners within each region.

PART II
INTRODUCTION TO ICRAN

'ICRAN is an innovative and dynamic global partnership of many of the world's leading coral reef science and conservation organizations. Its main objective is to halt and reverse the decline in health of the world's coral reefs. The partnership draws on its partners' investments in reef monitoring and management to create strategically linked actions across local, national, and global scales. ICRAN is thus the first partnership to respond to conservation needs at the global scale by recognizing both traditional and scientific perspectives of coral reef dynamics and respective social dependency. It seeks to put financial mechanisms in place that support the translation of findings into direct on-the-ground action throughout the world's major coral reef regions.'[6]

The International Coral Reef Action Network (ICRAN) [www.icran.org] is an active strategic alliance, which recognises that of the planet's 284,300 km^2 of coral reefs [1, 2], 70-80% are located in developing countries, with communities that derive their livelihoods from reef resources. With over 10% of the world's reefs already seriously degraded and a larger percentage being threatened [7], ICRAN focuses on strengthening the capacity of local communities to manage their marine and coastal resources sustainably through monitoring and communications [8], in order to mitigate and reverse coral reef decline.

In 1994, at the first conference of parties to the Convention on Biological Diversity (CBD), the International Coral Reef Initiative (ICRI) was first announced. Its mission is to address the plethora of threats leading to the rapid demise of reefs worldwide, help reverse current trends, and raise awareness about the ecosystem's decline in health [9]. The Initiative was to achieve this through its informal global partnership of world leaders (e.g. governments) and experts (e.g. NGOs, academic institutions and the private sector) on coral reefs.

At the first ICRI Workshop, held in the Philippines in June 1995, governments, donors, funding agencies, development organisations, NGOs, the scientific community, and private sector developed a 'Framework for Action,' a strategy document aimed at achieving sustainable management of coral reefs and related ecosystems [9]. They also endorsed the ICRI's 'Call to Action,' a policy statement by the international community intended to draw attention to 'the threats to coral reefs and their significance to humankind' [9]. ICRAN was established in 2000 in recognition of the need for research and management efforts to be coordinated across all relevant institutions in order to carry out ICRI's urgent recommendations to save the world's reefs.

The Network was set up by its founding partners (UNEP, WorldFish Centre (previously the International Centre for Living Aquatic Resources Management, (ICLARM)), World Resources Institute (WRI), UNEP-World Conservation Monitoring Centre (UNEP-WCMC), Global Coral Reef Monitoring Network (GCRMN), ICRI Secretariat, Coral Reef Alliance (CORAL)) as an innovative and dynamic global partnership of coral reef experts from both scientific and conservation organisations [6, 10]. The action phase of ICRAN was launched in 2001, with all activities made possible by an historic grant from then United Nations Foundation (UNF).

ICRAN's action plan recognises the importance of scientific, traditional, cultural, and economic aspects of conservation needs [6]. Findings are translated into direct on-the-ground action throughout the world's major coral reef regions, as well as at the regional and international levels [6], by means of a strategy that includes alternative livelihoods, training, capacity-building and the exchange of scientific, economic, traditional and social information [4]. In so doing, it puts into practice the notion that the overall success of Agenda 21 (a global programme of action and strategy document for sustainable development) depends significantly on dialogue and the development of a consensus between all local and national stakeholders [9].

Mission

ICRAN's current mission is based on three key interlinked components: (1) reef management, (2) global coral reef monitoring and assessment, and (3) communications and knowledge dissemination. UNEP, through its Regional Seas programmes, coordinates the reef management component of ICRAN in the Wider Caribbean, Eastern Africa, the South Pacific, and East Asian Seas region [11] (Table 1).

Reef management – Through local outreach, ICRAN assists local communities and coral reef managers by providing support and resources to enhance their management capacity and build on successfully implemented techniques. In addition to support provided at a local level, ICRAN offers a forum that allows for community experiences and knowledge to be extended to other interested coral reef managers and policy makers worldwide.

Global coral reef monitoring and assessment – By building on new and existing scientific data, learning from traditional local knowledge and the lessons of practical experiences, ICRAN partners are:

- continuing to develop ReefBase (www.reefbase.org) – a global database supporting management of coral reefs;

- producing coral reef maps and gathering field data to update reports on the condition of coral reefs worldwide;

- developing risk assessments of coral reef resources;

- conducting socio-economic valuations of coral reefs, including fisheries and mariculture analyses; and

- expanding the global Reefs at Risk programme, a project which has developed a series of globally-consistent indicators of human pressure on coral reefs. These indicators evaluate pressure from coastal development, marine-based pollution, sedimentation from inland sources, and overexploitation of coral resources [12], focusing on specific threats and regions.

Communications and knowledge dissemination – The International Coral Reef Information Network (ICRIN) www.icrin.org/ – serves as the communications and public awareness arm of ICRI. The network serves to provide general coral reef information, as well as tools and resources, based on data and reports from monitoring and assessment projects carried under ICRAN, to ICRAN partners, other key stakeholders, scientists, and policy makers at an international, regional, and local level. The ICRAN assessment and information dissemination activities are designed to produce and make available the knowledge needed to empower decision-makers to develop and implement policies for the sustainable management of coral reefs [10].

Table 1 – Demonstration sites (sites with proven ability to manage their coral reefs) and target sites (sites where best practices implemented at demonstration sites can be adopted) in the Caribbean, Eastern Africa, East Asia and South Pacific.

Region	Demonstration sites	Target sites
Caribbean	Hol Chan Marine Reserve (Belize)	Providencia (Colombia)
	Bonaire Marine Park (Bonaire)	Punta Frances (Cuba)
	Sian Ka'an Biosphere Reserve (Mexico)	Parque del Este (Dominican Republic)
	Soufriere Marine Management Area (St Lucia)	Portland Bight and Negril (Jamaica)
		Bucoo Marine Park (Tobago)
		Los Roques (Venezuela)
Eastern Africa	Malindi and Watamu Marine National Park and Reserve (Kenya)	
	Nosy Atafana Marine Park (Madagascar)	
	The Cousin Island Marine Protected Area (Seychelles)	
	Ste Anne Marine Park (Seychelles)	
	Dar es Salaam Marine Reserve (DMRS) (Tanzania)	
East Asia	Bunaken Island (Indonesia)	Ninh Thuan (Vietnam)
	Mo Koh Surin (Thailand)	Sanya (China)
	Apo Island Marine Reserve (Philippines)	Koh Rong (Cambodia)
	Komodo Island (Indonesia)	Gili Islands (Indonesia)
South Pacific	Samoa MPA Project – Savai' and Upolu Islands (Samoa)	
	Jaluit Atoll Marine Conservation Area (Marshall Islands)	
	Sustainable Management of Aquarium Harvesting Operations – Vitu Levu and Vanu Levu (Fiji)	Coral Gardens Project – Langa Langa Lagoon, Malafe Island (Solomon Islands)
	Coral Gardens Project – Cuvu Tikina (Coral Coast) (Fiji)	Tokelau Marine Conservation Area (Tokelau)

PART III
INTRODUCTION TO REGIONAL SEAS

The UNEP Regional Seas Programme, initiated in 1974, is a global programme that engages governments to focus on specific regional actions needed to control causes of environmental degradation as well as the mitigation or elimination of its consequences through the sustainable management of shared marine and coastal resources [13]. It has been identified by governments as the key regional mechanism for the implementation of ICRI [9].

At present the programme includes 13 Regional Seas programmes, the Mediterranean, Red Sea and Gulf of Aden, the Regional Organization for the Protection of the Marine Environment (ROPME) Sea Area (Kuwait region), Wider Caribbean, East Asian Seas, Southeast Pacific, Western and Central Africa, Eastern Africa, South Pacific, Black Sea, Northwest Pacific Action Plan, South Asian Seas, Northeast Pacific, and with the upper Southwest Atlantic in development [14]. There are also five partner seas programmes: Antarctic, Arctic, Caspian Sea, Oslo and Paris Commission (OSPAR) for the Northeast Atlantic and Helsinki Commission (HELCOM) for the Baltic [14, 15]. Overall, the programme links more than 140 coastal states and territories [14].

The Governing Council of UNEP has called for the development of regional action plans (prescriptions for sound environmental management [15]), formulated according to the needs and environmental challenges of a given region, as perceived by the governments concerned [16, 17]. Action plans should also recognise the human and financial capacity of partaking national institutions and be based on a region's socio-economic and political situation [13]. Regional action plans (Table 2) for those involving countries with coral reefs) further promote the parallel development of regional legal agreements and of programme activities, by linking assessments of the quality of the marine environment and causes for its deterioration with actions towards the sustainable management of marine and coastal resources [13].

West to East: North-East Pacific South-East Pacific Wider Caribbean Upper South-West Atlantic West & Central Africa Mediterranean Black Sea Eastern Africa Red Sea & Gulf of Aden ROPME Sea Area South Asian Seas East Asian Seas North-West Pacific South Pacific Partner programmes: Arctic North-East Atlantic Baltic Sea Caspian Sea Antarctic

Although the specific activities for any region are dependent upon the needs and priorities of that region, all regional action plans, which have to be formally adopted by all governments of a given region, are structured in a similar way. The Earth Summit/UN Conference on Environment and Development (UNCED)/ World Summit on Sustainable Development (WSSD) held in Johannesburg (2002), in many ways, helped shape the work agenda and priorities (Water, Energy, Health, Agriculture, and Biodiversity (WEHAB)) of the various programmes [27]. Action plans usually include the following independent components [35, 36]:

1. *Environmental Assessment* – Causes of environmental degradation are monitored and evaluated to estimate the magnitude and impact of ecological problems in the region. These findings are then used to prioritize future action.

2. *Environmental Management* – Activities aimed at curbing existing environmental problems and preventing the development of new ones.

3. *Environmental Legislation* – The legal framework for cooperative regional and national actions is provided by an umbrella regional convention, elaborated through specific technical protocols.

4. *Institutional Arrangements* – Upon adoption of an action plan, governments agree to act as the permanent or interim secretariat of the action plan.

5. *Financial Arrangements* – UNEP, together with selected UN agencies and other organizations, provides catalytic support, or so called 'seed money,' in the early stages of regional programmes. However, as programmes develop, it is expected that the governments of the region will come to assume full financial responsibility for the activities implemented.

Some of the priority issues being addressed by the Regional Seas agreements include [36]:

- *Ecosystems and biodiversity*, with emphasis being placed on coral reefs, considered to be among the most productive of all natural ecosystems, but facing a wide array of serious threats; and coastal wetlands including mangrove forests and salt marshes;

- *Living resources,* with fish, molluscs and crustaceans, representing major food sources for subsistence communities around the world, but many of these populations now being threatened by overexploitation;

- *Land-based sources of pollution,* where municipal, industrial, and agricultural wastes, as well as run-off constitute 80% of all marine pollution;

- *Coastal development,* caused by expanding coastal populations, which are reshaping the coastline and causing the decline of habitats and their associated species.

Although overall coordination of the Regional Seas programmes is guaranteed by the Regional Seas Co-ordinating Office of UNEP in Nairobi, the success of the programme critically depends on the political commitment of the governments concerned. The regional programmes are implemented at the national and regional level by relevant organizations dealing with particular issues, many of which represent common concerns of other regional programmes.

Today, UNEP is developing a new strategic action programme to foster collaboration among Regional Seas Conventions and Actions Plans and their global counterparts. Key elements of this programme include commitment, participation, sustainability, and partnership. The strategy calls in particular for close coordination with the Global Plan of Action for the Protection of the Marine Environment from Land-based Sources of Pollution (UNEP GPA), Multilateral Environmental Agreements (MEAs), ICRI, ICRAN, the Global International Water Assessment (GIWA) and the Global Plan of Action for Marine Mammals. Cooperation should also be reinforced with international organizations such as the International Maritime Organization (IMO), the Intergovernmental Oceanographic Commission of the United Nations Educational, Scientific, and Cultural Organization (IOC of UNESCO), and the Food and Agriculture Organization of the United Nations (FAO). Moreover, participation in the Global Assessment of the State of the Marine Environment (GMA) and in the Barbados Programme of Action for the Sustainable Development of Small Island Developing States should be fostered [13].

PART IV
INTERNATIONAL TROPICAL MARINE ECOSYSTEMS MANAGEMENT SYMPOSIUM 2

ICRAN SESSION WORKSHOP REPORT: ROLE OF MARINE PROTECTED AREAS IN MANAGEMENT

The Second International Tropical Marine Ecosystems Management Symposium (ITMEMS 2) held in Manila, Philippines, 24–27 March 2003, brought together 200 people from 36 countries. The meeting consisted of 20 workshops, which considered priority issues and problems of management identified through a questionnaire that had been sent to managers from all coral reef regions of the world, early in the conference planning process [37]. Backgrounds varied from managers, scientists, private sector, NGOs, to development and funding agencies, reflecting a broad range of experience. The aim of the symposium was to review the issues facing tropical marine ecosystems as well as progress to date, and share and discuss lessons learned in implementing the ICRI Framework for Action. A specific objective of the symposium was also to provide an opportunity for managers to engage in multidisciplinary discussions to identify gaps and priorities for future management action [37].

ICRAN hosted and chaired the session entitled 'The Role of Protected Areas in Management'. In this session, managers and practitioners from a number of ICRAN sites shared their experiences, described lessons learned, challenges faced from their particular park, and discussed how the ICRAN network can make a contribution towards addressing the site priorities and needs, as well as future learning opportunities. The discussions and recommendations proposed by the participants in this session were promoted by eight presentations from four ICRAN regions (Table 3, in bold). An additional number of studies have

Table 3 – Case studies discussed in this report. The ones listed in bold were presented at ITMEMS 2, those in normal font had been accepted, but, due to unforeseen circumstances, the authors were unable to attend the conference.

CARIBBEAN	Community-Based Coastal Resource Management and Marine Biodiversity Conservation; Lessons from Punta Allen, Sian Ka'an Biosphere Reserve, Mexico
	Capacity Building for Marine Protected Area Management: The Case of the UNEP-CEP Training of Trainers Programme
	Management plan of 'Banco Chinchorro' Biosphere Reserve: A case study of Concerted Rules and Zoning with Stakeholders
	Admission Fees: Opportunities and Challenges of Using Admission Fees as a Funding Source at a Small Scale, Tourism Dependant MPA. Case Study of the Bonaire National Marine Park, Bonaire
	Strengthening Relationships: The Case of the Soufriere Marine Management Area (SMMA), Saint Lucia
	Community Policing and the 'Culture of System-Beating': The Honorary Game Wardens and Fisheries Inspectors of the Portland Bight Protected Area, Jamaica, West Indies
	Conflict Resolution Between Inter-Sectoral Stakeholders for the Buccoo Reef Marine Park Coastal Zone in Tobago: The Pigeon Point Case Study
EAST AFRICA	Implementing ICRAN Activities at the Malindi/Watamu MPA Complex Demonstration Site, Kenya
	Challenges and Opportunities in Managing Marine Reserves Surrounded by Poor Population and Urban Settings. Case study of the Dar es Salaam Marine Reserves System, Tanzania
EAST ASIA	Solution strategies of the Alternative Income Increase in Gili Matra Marine Natural Recreation Park (GM-MNRP) West Nusa Tenggara Province, Indonesia
	Bunaken National Park Co-Management Initiative
SOUTH PACIFIC	Multiple-Use Management Plan for Whole of Atoll Management: Jaluit Atoll Marine Conservation Area Management Plan
	Coral Transplantation and Restocking to Accelerate the Recovery of Coral Reef Habitats and Fisheries Resources within No-Take Marine Protected Areas: Hands-on Approaches to Support Community-Based Coral Reef Management

been included in this report as these had been accepted for presentation at the symposium, but, due to unforeseen circumstances/political tensions, the presenters were unable to attend the conference (Table 3, normal font).

Results of the ICRAN workshop

The presentations illustrated activities throughout the four coral reef regions, highlighting capacity building, the development of management plans, resource use conflicts, private sector involvement and partnerships, as well as alternative livelihoods. In addition to providing a global forum for ICRAN global partners to present their regional activities, the ICRAN session allowed participants to exchange information about experiences, and get a wider perspective on the project as a whole. It also presented ICRAN with the opportunity to showcase the successes and challenges of a project implemented on a local scale via a global network.

The following set of questions guided the discussion that followed on from the presentations:

1. What additional role can ICRAN play in the short and long-term to strengthen the capacity of communities and MPAs to manage their tropical marine resources?

2. With emphasis on peer-to-peer interactions and ICRAN's innovative approach of focusing its efforts on sustainability of reefs and community livelihoods, are there significant benefits to participating in a global learning framework?

3. What additional learning opportunities should ICRAN be contributing to, and promoting, in an effort to strengthen learning experience and framework through peer-to-peer networks?

4. Do the projects and priorities of ICRAN fulfil the needs at the site level? What should the priorities of ICRAN be?

5. Can a global initiative respond adequately to what a local coastal community would define as sustainability?

6. What lessons have been learned through the formation and implementation of an ICRAN network that is based upon information and experience sharing?

The discussions addressed issues of stakeholder involvement and conflicting use of marine resources, a recurring theme through all ICRAN sites. Other concerns highlighted the still prevalent use of destructive fishing practices, as well as the lack of enforcement and monitoring in all of the four coral reef regions. Participants also drew attention to the need for greater integration of traditional management systems (e.g. traditionally closed areas) with so called 'modern' systems, particularly in the South Pacific region. Lack of awareness of the importance of MPAs, lack of management capacity, lack of alternative income opportunities, and lack of stakeholder involvement in management planning still threaten the success and effectiveness of many marine reserves.

Participants also discussed how material presented could be used to highlight valuable lessons learned through ICRAN, what management initiatives ICRAN can provide elsewhere in the world, and how ICRAN should encourage sustainable practices. A number of 'lessons learned' were brought up by a number of participants. These included amongst others:

- Stakeholders are to be involved at all stages of MPA planning and management and feel empowered.

- Public awareness and education campaigns at all levels are crucial to the success of a MPA.

- The periodic review of training materials is important; follow-up training courses for MPA managers would improve capacity building and communication needs to be carefully targeted to individual user groups.

- When zoning a tropical marine national park, active involvement of primary user groups and a spirit of compromise are crucial to success. Zonation schemes should be kept relatively simple, with clearly demarcated boundaries. In addition to the need for MPAs to be geographically well defined, user rights have to be made clear.

- The most important aspects of successful implementation of a park user fee system are (a) active involvement of the tourism sector in the design of the system, and (b) earmarking of revenues for conservation and related education, as well as outreach and monitoring activities, in order to gain widespread tourist acceptance.

- Involvement of the private sector in co-management of MPAs is highly beneficial. Once potential business competitors focus on the benefits of cooperating to protect the resources in the MPA upon which their income depends, they become one of the strongest proponents of good management and bring considerable financial and human resources to the table.

- While multi-stakeholder co-management is clearly an effective strategy, a firm enforcement system is critical to achieving natural resource management goals. In the Indonesian context, multi-stakeholder patrols involving both trained security officers and local villagers have proven highly effective.

- Alternative income opportunities for local communities should be developed to lessen the pressure on marine resource harvesting. However, 'alternative livelihood programmes,' aimed at stakeholders currently involved in destructive activities in the coastal zone, are ineffective and largely rejected by local communities. Community conservation/improvement programmes should focus on rewarding those that have chosen sustainable livelihoods, while those that persevere with destructive activities should be dealt with by a strong enforcement system.

Finally, workshop participants proposed the following recommendations:

- Donor agencies must recognise the need for, and importance of, long-term projects.

- Global initiatives should be used to leverage funding for capacity building in local communities.

- Small amounts of funding can go a long way, i.e. donors do not need to invest large amounts to achieve good results.

- International programmes need to recognise that local communities have great pride in working with them.

- Mechanisms should be designed to foster self-sufficiency and local counterpart involvement.

- Exit strategies are needed for self-sufficiency, e.g. transfer of leadership and funding to local agencies and communities.

- 'Keep up the good work' – managers should continue their good performance to obtain additional funds, and not become complacent with seed funding.

- Need for continued support of exchange programmes (cross-visits), e.g. community to community, peer to peer.

- Increase networking at all levels (managers, cross communities) and establishment of a managers-dedicated network.

- Need for specific training for managers, e.g. Training of Trainers Programme.

- Networks should facilitate the compilation of lessons learned/best practices, taking into account the context in which they worked, and disseminate the information.

- Evaluation of activities is needed to determine level of success – need for documentation, useful information for donors.

More detailed results and discussion of lessons learned from these case studies, and selected others, can be found under the following regional chapters.

PART V
THE WIDER CARIBBEAN REGION

The Wider Caribbean region (ICRAN), home to about 300 million people [38], encompasses an area of 4.31 million km2 including twelve continental countries bordering the Wider Caribbean basin, 14 islands as well as 7 dependent territories [39].

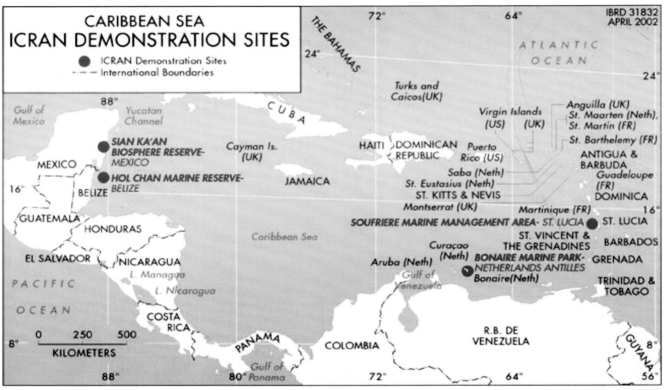

Wider Caribbean Region. Source: ICRAN

The Region – Habitat, Population and Economic Characteristics

Coral reef (the Caribbean region hosts a little under 8% of the world's total reef area [2]), seagrass, mangrove, swamp, and coastal lagoon habitats are reasonably well developed in all Wider Caribbean countries and present relatively high biodiversity [40]. The region includes the Mesoamerican Barrier Reef System (MBRS), second largest in the world, which extends through Mexico, Belize, Guatemala, and Honduras.

It is a complex region exhibiting wide disparities in the population levels, degree of economic development, capacity to monitor and manage ecological resources, and access to wealth and natural resources (e.g. Puerto Rico versus Haiti) [41]. Throughout the region, island communities are heavily reliant on marine and coastal systems for their livelihoods. Besides providing benefits such as coastal protection, these ecosystems employ large numbers of people and provide major sources of income through tourism and fishing.

In contrast, in Mesoamerica, until recently, coastal activities have typically played a minor role, with national economies being mostly based on agriculture and small industries [42]. However, in recent years, coastal and cruise tourism has become one of the driving economic forces in most areas, particularly in Belize and Mexico [42].

Through the development of the MBRS programme, funded by the Global Environment Facility (GEF), and numerous local and international NGOs' initiatives, conservation efforts are aimed mainly at forming a representative network of MPAs, developing sustainable tourism and fisheries management, improving watershed management, and generating sustainable long-term funding [42]. Through these programmes

Coastal tourism in Mexico. © Colette Wabnitz

and the soon to be implemented, complementary, and supporting ICRAN Mesoamerican Reef Alliance, capacity in the region is expected to increase, and it is hoped that resource levels and habitat health will recover.

Major anthropogenic impacts in the Caribbean region stem mainly from land-based sources of pollution (sewage, agricultural discharge, industrial effluents); sedimentation due to poor land use and unsustainable forestry practices; land reclamation; unregulated coastal development; urban expansion; shipping [43]; dumping [43]; physical damage due to increasing tourism activities; and serious over-exploitation of resources such as fish, molluscs, and crustaceans [44]. Fisheries of commercially important (i.e., high-value) species (e.g., conch, lobster, and groupers) have been particularly overexploited. In addition to anthropogenic impacts, reefs in the Mesoamerican and Eastern Caribbean region have suffered from a series of significant natural disturbances (e.g. repeated hurricane impact in 2000, 2001 and 2002). Belize, for example, experienced up to 75% losses of its corals due to such disturbances [42]. Overall, the region's marine and coastal resources are exhibiting continued decline and evidence of stress [45]. More than 60% of the region's coral reefs are under threat, with entire reefs having been decimated by disease [2].

With most countries only possessing limited opportunities for the expansion of their economies, tourism (including the cruise industry which hosts 50% of the cruising passengers of the world) is a large and fast-growing industrial sector [43]. However, uncontrolled coastal tourism development poses potential threats, as it can put enormous pressure on a very limited area. On the other hand, tourism has the potential to contribute to environmental protection and conservation by raising awareness of environmental values and serving as a tool to finance protection of natural areas, thus increasing their economic importance [46].

In areas where legislative frameworks are in force and management of resources effective, some of the pressures have been removed successfully (partly through the implementation of MPAs) [41]. However, for islands where economic circumstances remain unstable and monitoring and/or management activities of biological resources are severely limited (e.g. Cuba and Haiti), and in countries where conservation and/or sustainable management plans have not been properly enforced (e.g. Cuba, Jamaica, Dominican Republic), conditions have worsened [41, 45]. The establishment of MPAs is still lauded as one of the best ways to assist with the conservation of coastal and marine ecosystems in the region [47]. However, with over 300 coastal and marine protected areas declared or established in the Wider Caribbean, about 70% are only partially managed or not being managed at all [10]. Most of these areas suffer from inadequate legislation and/or lack of enforcement of existing laws, lack of financial sustainability and trained personnel, thus often not meeting the objectives for which they were originally established.

The UNEP Caribbean Regional Co-ordinating Unit (CAR/RCU) – Secretariat

The Convention for the Protection and Development of the Marine Environment of the Wider Caribbean Region, The Cartagena Convention, adopted in 1983, served as the legal framework for the development of the Caribbean Environment Programme (CEP) [48]. Although part of UNEP, the CEP is administered by the countries and territories that adopted the Caribbean Action Plan in 1981 (see Table 2). Three protocols, the Protocol on Cooperation in Combating Oil Spills, the Protocol on Specially Protected Areas and Wildlife (SPAW, signed in Jamaica in 1990 and which entered into force 10 years later) and the Protocol on Land Based Sources of Marine Pollution (LBS protocol) supplement the Cartagena Convention. The CEP's main activities concentrate on the implementation of the protocols through government and institutional capacity support, information management and exchange, and on environmental education and training through workshops and the production of relevant materials [44].

UNEP CAR/RCU, founded in 1986 and located in Kingston, Jamaica, assists the CEP and serves as its secretariat [10]. As a sub-programme of UNEP's Regional Seas Programme, it is directly responsible to the region's member governments, whilst being administered by UNEP Headquarters (Nairobi). Reports and publications disseminated by CAR/RCU staff generally present the results of activities facilitated by CEP, coordinated by CAR/RCU and implemented through national and technical focal points, experts in scientific, academic, regional, and sub-regional institutions, and individual consultants [10].

The CAR/RCU has four sub-programmes:

1. *The Assessment and Management of Environmental Pollution* (AMEP) *Programme* provides regional coordination for the implementation of the LBS Protocol and the Oil Spills Protocol. It supports activities needed to establish measures required to prevent, reduce, and control marine pollution and to assist in the development of integrated environmental planning and management of marine and coastal areas. [19].

2. *The SPAW Programme* supports schemes aimed at protecting and managing fragile and highly valuable natural marine and coastal habitats and their resources. Such activities consist mainly of assisting with the establishment and proper management of protected areas, by promoting sustainable management (and use) of habitats and species to prevent their endangerment, and by providing support to local governments. This includes the development of regional capacity to coordinate efforts for information exchange, training, and technical assistance in support of national biodiversity conservation efforts [49].

3. *The Education Training and Awareness Programme* is responsible for developing ecological awareness as well as research, technical, and managerial capacity to ensure effective environmental management of Caribbean States and Territories [50].

4. *CEPNET* acts to promote information and data networks both in terms of electronic information management systems (e.g. databases) and networking expertise [51].

ICRAN at the Caribbean level

Through its active involvement in the ICRI process, the Wider Caribbean holds a series of priority opportunities for ICRAN, a group of trained trainers on MPAs management, and the means to identify candidate sites and target communities [50]. Some of the selected sites in the region include [50] (see also Table 1):

- *Soufriere Marine Management Area (SMMA)*, St. Lucia: 'to demonstrate successful conflict resolution, community participation in planning and management, and effectiveness of zoning practices'.

- *Hol Chan Marine Reserve*, Belize: 'to demonstrate successful alternative livelihoods for fishers and their involvement in monitoring and enforcement of regulations'.

- *Bonaire National Marine Park*: 'to demonstrate sustainable financing and successful private sector participation by hoteliers and dive operators'.

- *Sian Ka'an Biosphere Reserve,* Mexico: 'to demonstrate successful practices in a multipurpose protected area with both active fisheries and tourism'.

To ensure sustainable management and conservation of resources, ICRAN has developed a set of regional activities to address the lack of sustainable financing and capacity; often unsustainable fishing and tourism practices; and lack of coral reef monitoring activities in the region. Such activities include [50]:

- The preparation of a Regional Reefs at Risk report (map-based indicator of threats to coral reefs) for the Caribbean, in cooperation with WRI, and the support of UNEP, World Fish Centre, UNEP-WCMC and GCRMN [52]. A preliminary Threat Assessment Workshop with Partners and regional stakeholders was held in Miami in October 2002. The Regional reefs at Risk Caribbean report was launched September 2004 in Montego Bay, Jamaica during the 11the Intergovernmental Meeting on the Action Plan for the Caribbean Envrionment Programme and the 8th Meeting of the Contracting Parties to the Cartagena Convention that was attended by government officials and scientists. The meeting will also serve as the launch of the report's companion web site at http://reefsatrisk.wri.org."

- The development of focused and effective public awareness activities (e.g. campaigns, materials) in collaboration with CORAL/ICRIN to raise awareness amongst target communities.

- The support of the existing UNEP/CEP Training of Trainers programme on all aspects of MPA management. Courses have been held in English in Saba (1999) and St. Lucia(2002), and in Spanish in the Dominican Republic (2000) and most recently in Florida (2004).

- The development of low-cost, standardized coral reef monitoring activities among all participating sites and MPAs. This will include involvement in GCRMN, the Caribbean Coastal Marine Productivity Programme (CARICOMP), ReefBase, ReefCheck, and the Atlantic and Gulf Rapid Reef Assessment (AGRRA). ICRAN is to provide on-the-job training to enhance government and community capacity in basic coral-reef monitoring and assessment techniques. ReefCheck Training and Coral Reef Monitoring activities have recently been carried out in Les Arcadins, Haiti, in September, 2003. Also in September, a ReefCheck training workshop, followed by data collection in the Negril Marine Park, was facilitated by the Jamaican Coral Reef Monitoring Network (JCRMN) and led by the Caribbean Coastal Data Centre (CCDC). A similar training was held in the Portland Bight Protected Area, Jamaica.

- The update and analysis of UNEP-WCMC's global database of MPAs and the Centre's coral-reef maps to produce an assessment of the role of MPAs in the protection of coral reefs.

- The development of ReefBase's capacity (a global coral reef database) by the World Fish Centre, together with GCRMN and other monitoring and field data programmes, to operate as a management-information support system.

- The analysis of various sources of information to develop a set of standardized variables best used to estimate the economic value of coral reefs. This project is to be implemented with the cooperation of the World Fish Centre. Moreover, an analytical review of national policies for sustainable management and policies that adversely affect reefs will be conducted.

Details and outputs of the activities can be found at www.icran.org.

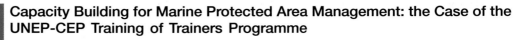

CASE STUDIES

Capacity Building for Marine Protected Area Management: the Case of the UNEP-CEP Training of Trainers Programme

Malden Miller and Alessandra Vanzella-Khouri

Issues and topics covered

Stakeholder Involvement, Empowerment and Community Support

Capacity Building, Public Awareness and Education

Background

One of the main reasons for the management failure of marine reserves in the Caribbean is the lack of capacity demonstrated by MPA managers. In the past, although some training has been made available to MPA managers of the region, it has been thematic, relatively infrequent and short-term. This problem was also highlighted at the 'International Workshop on Framework for Future Training in Marine and Coastal Protected Area Management' organized by the Netherlands-based Coastal Zone Management Centre (CZMC) and held in Manila, Philippines, in 1997. All participants stressed and endorsed the need for additional training of trainers, and the development of training modules addressing issues of MPA management.

To tackle the issue of lack of capacity, the UNEP-CAR/RCU launched a 'Training of Trainers' programme for MPA managers. Through structured workshops, managers are not only trained in all aspects of MPA management but also taught how to conduct local and tailored training activities in their respective MPAs. This approach includes regional two-week courses, followed by local training sessions, which the trained managers commit to undertake upon completion of the regional courses. Development of the curriculum modules and manual was primarily supported by the Netherlands Ministry of Transport, Public Works and Management, under the Netherlands Government Programme through its CZMC. The activities are intended to support the implementation of the Action Programme of the Jakarta Mandate of the Convention on Biological Diversity (CBD). Assistance for implementation of the programme was also provided by the World Bank, the US Government, The Nature Conservancy (TNC) and the UN Foundation through ICRAN. Within the operational context of ICRAN, this programme is seen as a critical contribution towards sustainable management of coral reefs in the Wider Caribbean and the Network has contributed to its initial launch and development.

The Training of Trainers Programme

The Programme included the development of a course manual and modules in MPA management on the basis of a regional needs assessment undertaken within the Wider Caribbean region, by UNEP, during 1998. An experts meeting was held in December 1998 to finalize the course design.

The training manual contains a total of eight modules covering the following specific subject areas:

1. Training and Communication Skills
2. The Nature of the Marine Environment
3. Uses and Threats to the Marine Environment and its Resources
4. MPAs Overview
5. Participatory Planning
6. MPA Planning
7. MPA Management
8. Research and Monitoring

Since the inception of the 'Training of Trainers' programme, three regional courses have been offered and a total of 11 local training activity sessions implemented, for which assistance was provided to the participating countries. The first workshop, aimed at English speaking countries, was conducted from 2-13 November 1999 in Saba, Netherlands Antilles. Ten MPA managers participated in the course and subsequently organized local training activities within their respective MPAs, benefiting a total of 121 MPA staff and practitioners at the local level. The second regional course was held in Bayahibe, Dominican Republic, from 1-13 May 2000, engaging 15 Spanish-speaking Caribbean MPA managers, who subsequently trained a total of 126 MPA and coastal zone practitioners. A third course was held in Soufriere, St. Lucia, from 27 October - 10 November 2002, for twelve MPA Managers whose proposals to conduct follow up training are now complete. The most recent course was held in Florida from the 27 January - 10 February 2004 at the Florida Keys Marine Laboratory, conducted again in Spanish and coordinated by The Nature Conservancy (TNC).

Course Objectives

The goal of the Training of Trainers Programme is to build a team of MPA managers in the Wider Caribbean able to design and deliver quality training activities at the local level, ultimately resulting in improved MPA management throughout the region.

The specific objectives of the course were:

1. To introduce MPA managers to the theory of adult education and relevant teaching methods;

2. To provide participants with additional knowledge, skills, materials, and information to improve MPA management in their own countries; and

3. To stimulate the exchange of information and experiences, as well as communication among trainees and trainers.

In addition, priority areas of the Training of Trainers Programme were identified for further assistance.

Expected Results

Results expected to be derived from the organized regional courses and local training activities included the following:

- A comprehensive 'Train the Trainers' Course Manual and Modules, also available on CD-ROM in both English and Spanish, to assist in replication of the training sessions undertaken at the local level. In addition to practical exercises, it includes theory of MPA management, and reference materials;

- An increase in the number of trained trainers (MPA managers) exhibiting skills in management, planning, training, and communication;

- An increase in the number of trained MPA staff in general, as a result of local training activities undertaken by MPA managers who have participated in regional level courses;

- A widely disseminated analysis of successful approaches to ICM and MPA management, to act as the basis for the development of guidelines for other MPAs in the region. It is hoped that this process will increase awareness and knowledge related to MPA management, particularly for managers and other coral reef stakeholders;

- A report assessing the impact of the training programme; and

- Recommendations for further assistance.

These results should assist participants to manage their habitats and resources in a sustainable manner through MPAs, co-management, and participatory planning. The training programme has also resulted in increased capacity and helped to raise the level of skills of MPA managers and their staff. Through local training programmes, this should in turn result in higher capacities throughout the Wider Caribbean Region.

Outstanding Challenges

A key difficulty in the implementation of the programme was that some MPA managers, who had attended the regional training workshops, were slow or ineffective in developing and implementing the training activities they had committed to. This resulted in delays in the implementation of training courses, and had a negative impact on the project as a whole. The response of the UNEP-CAR/RCU response was proactive in offering assistance and additional time for the preparation of training proposals. However, follow-up and execution of local activities often occurred only after repeated requests from CAR/RCU. In an effort to speed up the process of local training development, participants in the third regional course were required to finalize draft proposals of activities to be undertaken, prior to the end of the programme.

A key lesson learned during programme implementation was that the original timetable and workplan were too ambitious, requiring the agreement of project extensions. In the future, similar activities will need to develop a more realistic timetable, taking into account the limited resources and capacities of the participating MPAs and countries. This issue restricted the MPAs' ability to have fully active and productive participation in the project activities. Moreover, the majority of MPAs had few staff with the necessary management skills to participate, resulting in limited time and resources for the additional required local training activities. It is critical not to attempt to accomplish too much, as the quality and the real benefits of the project outputs might suffer as a consequence. In addition, despite the selection criteria used to determine the most appropriate applicants, the process was insufficient in securing committed candidates for participation in the training courses. Future initiatives will require more cautious and considered selection processes.

Self-Assessment of Success and Stakeholder Participation

The following objectives of the programme were realized:

- Successul organization of four regional workshops;

- Development of a training manual and CD-Rom in Spanish and English;

- Provision of grants for local training activities;

- Implementation of follow-up training activities in twelve participating countries.

Although the project did not include a public awareness component, positive results were measured in terms of increased awareness amongst MPA staff and other stakeholders about existing MPA training programmes and MPA needs. This was evidenced by the increased number of requests CAR-RCU received for information on MPAs following the training initiatives. At a regional level, programmes were primarily intended for MPA managers and/or senior MPA staff. At a local level, training courses allowed for the participation of a wide array of local stakeholders, such as dive-site operators. Regional and local training courses were also evaluated by both participants and course instructors to measure strengths and weaknesses. In addition, TNC undertook a comprehensive assessment of courses held in Spanish-speaking countries to determine their impact and provided support to ensure that needs of regional stakeholders were met. This evaluation identified priority areas of the programme that would benefit from further assistance.

Overall, the initiative seems to have had a sustainable impact on the capacity of MPA staff throughout the Caribbean, with follow-up training courses providing an effective indicator of local capacity-building success. In the long run, these skills will have positive repercussions on the decision-making process within the region's MPAs and contribute towards the long-term sustainability of the initiative.

LESSONS LEARNED

Stakeholder Involvement, Empowerment, and Community Support

- To maximize benefits and ensure successful implementation of all activities, a cautious and considered selection process for workshop participants should be developed involving individuals whose economic interests are dependent on effective coastal and marine management.

Capacity Building

- Successful training of trainers' courses should be replicated throughout regions and in different regions, making use of materials, training manuals, and lessons learned from previous courses, with local adaptation.

- Realistic timetables and workplans should be developed, taking into account the limited resources and capacities of participating MPAs and countries.

- Clear achievable goals should be set.

- Draft proposals of activities implemented at local MPA level should be finalized **prior** to the end of the trainers' programme.

- Training manuals should be regularly updated with new data, to make sure information is kept as relevant as possible. Facilitators for each module are to be made responsible for this.

- Regular comprehensive evaluations of the programme should be undertaken.

- Increased capacity among MPA managers and staff can lead to improved management and planning skills contributing to the long-term sustainability of the initiative and of resource use.

Community-Based Coastal Resource Management and Marine Biodiversity Conservation; Lessons from Punta Allen, Sian Ka'an Biosphere Reserve, Mexico

Oscar Alvarez

Background

In the language of the Mayan people, Sian Ka'an means 'Origin of the Sky' [53]. Located on the East coast of the Yucatán peninsula in the State of Quintana Roo, Mexico, this 5,280 km² biosphere reserve contains tropical forests, mangroves, and marshes, as well as a large marine section with seagrass beds and coastal lagoons (1,200 km²) intersected by a barrier reef (120 km in length) [53, 54]. These communities provide habitat for a remarkably rich flora and fauna. The reserve's coral reefs are famous for their sport fish populations of tarpon, bonefish, snook, and permit [55].

<table>
<tr><td>

Issues and topics covered

Stakeholder Involvement, Empowerment, and Community Support

Zoning and Conflict Resolution

Partnerships for Management

Tourism and Sustainable Development

</td></tr>
</table>

Sian Ka'an was declared a national biosphere reserve in 1986 by the Comisión Nacional de Areas Naturales Protegidas (CONANP; Commission for Natural Protected Areas), a decentralized body of the Federal Government, recognised as an International Biosphere Reserve by the Man and the Biosphere (MAB) International Coordinating Council in late 1986, and inscribed on the UNESCO World Heritage List in 1987 [54]. The reserve is located in the least developed part of Quintana Roo, with a population of predominantly Mayan origin. There are reported to be about 800 permanent and 200 temporary residents living in the buffer zone along the coast, another 450 people residing in the Javier Rojo Gomez community on Punta Allen, and a further 50 at Punta Herrero [55]. The remainder live in settlements ('rancherias') scattered along the coast and in the forest [54]. Fishing constitutes the most important income-generation activity, followed by agriculture (maize and copra) [54]. The Caribbean spiny lobster, *Panulirus argus*, makes up the main catch (75%). Over the last 11 years, yearly landings have averaged 80 metric tons, the majority of which is exported to the United States and Japan [55].

The primary management goals of the Sian Ka'an Biosphere Reserve include the preservation of the area's physical integrity; sustainable use of natural resources; fostering of social integration; development of research and education initiatives; and establishment of a long-term self-supported financial framework for the reserve [55].

The reserve itself is divided into three zones:

1. A *core zone*, the most 'pristine' area, set aside for conservation purposes and limited research.

2. A *buffer zone*, which allows low human-impact activities and sustainable use of natural resources.

3. A *cooperation zone*, which includes the terrestrial areas and human settlements next to the reserve's boundary and where a range of natural resource management measures are applied.

Sian Ka'an Biosphere Reserve. © Jamie Oliver

Tourism activities began to develop in the 1970s, when beaches around Tulum, to the north of the reserve, started to attract foreign visitors [54]. For this reason, long-term conservation policies (although the management plan is currently under review) for the reserve mainly address tourism activities such as sport fishing, wildlife watching, snorkelling), nature walks, camping, and kayaking [55]. Although seen as a potentially important source of revenue, talks of further tourism expansion have raised concern, as visitor facilities have been extending apparently uncontrolled. Moreover, they present an increasing threat to the area's fragile ecosystem [54]. Over-fishing, due to the sprawl of urban centres and increased tourism demand, has led to drastic declines in natural resource numbers, in particular of lobsters. In addition to reductions in fish population sizes, year-round tourism has also meant that there has been a constant demand for seafood, at times driving fishermen to sell illegal sizes.

An ICRAN socio-economic study has recently been published that assesses the value of community-based management along the coast and provides a baseline towards a long-term monitoring programme.

Lobster Fishery

Initially, lobsters were being caught using primarily hook and line. In later years, the fishery developed the use of traps, and in 1969 the Cuban method of fishing for lobster using 'little houses,' or *casitas*, made of local resources (and/or concrete), and imitating the animal's natural shelter, was introduced. The latter system was later abandoned in favour of a more intensive hook-and-line fishery. In the north-eastern areas of the peninsula, this led to drastic declines in lobster stocks. However, in the Javier Rojo Gomez fishing cooperative, also known as Punta Allen, located in one of the two bays of the Sian Ka'an Biosphere Reserve, lobsters are still relatively abundant. This is chiefly attributable to the more informed attitude of local community members (nearly all of whom are members of the Vigia Chico Cooperative Society, established at the end of the 1950s) towards their environment and also, partly, to the favourable physical and biological conditions prevalent in the bay. The lobster fishery tends to be most active in the central part of the Bahia de la Ascension, which consists of shallow-water habitat rarely exceeding five metres in depth. A large number of reproductive lobsters are located in the deeper parts of the reef, around 40 metres and beyond, allowing them to grow to large sizes without being captured, and thus replenishing the fished stock.

Coral reef biodiversity in Sian Ka'an represents a major tourist attraction. © Oscar Alvarez

Punta Allen

At the end of the 1970s, when lobster fisheries started to decline and competition as well as conflict between fishermen increased, the cooperative decided to discuss the design of operative rules to regulate the fishery.

These rules consisted of the following:

1. Each fisherman was assigned a specific fishing ground, clearly delineated with buoys. The size of individual fishing grounds originally depended on the number of traps one fisherman could realistically deploy, leaving a number of gaps between individual areas. However, as the number of Cooperative members grew, increase in fishing effort was eventually capped.

2. Fishing grounds were allocated according to trust, reputation, seniority, and rank.

3. The Cuban fishing method, making use of casitas, was selected as the only fishing technique allowed.

4. The Cooperative was to market each fisherman's catch.

Lobster fisher and his catch.
© Oscar Alvarez

5. Lobsters captured in perfect condition were to be sold 'live'.

6. Minimum capture fees were introduced.

7. Reef formations were designated as restricted or no-take zones.

8. A ban was implemented for the capture of egg-carrying females and individuals below a certain size-limit.

9. The use of hooks and scuba equipment for fishing was prohibited.

10. All partners were to abide by the rules and participate in their implementation and amendment, if and when deemed necessary.

Fishing boats at Punta Allen. © Jamie Oliver

11. Partners found violating the rules were to receive graduated sanctions, depending on the severity and the context of the infraction, by the Cooperative Society and the federal government (Sian Ka'an Biosphere Reserve, Mexican Environmental Attorney General's Office (Procuraduría Federal de Protección al Ambiente - PROPEPA), Mexican Secretariat of Agriculture (Secretaría de Agricultura, Ganadería, Desarollo Rural, Pesca y Alimentación - SAGARPA)). Anyone found fishing in someone else's fishing ground, or caught with undersize and forbidden species, was to be evicted from the cooperative.

12. All fishermen were to acknowledge the rights of the Cooperative Society to apply its own rules, by way of any government institutions.

13. Membership to the Cooperative Society and the fishing grounds were only transferable by inheritance or when given to another partner within the Cooperative.

Mesoamerican Barrier Reef.
© Oscar Alvarez

Thus, although dealing with common property resources, and unlike in the north-eastern part of the peninsula where unregulated fishing led to the 'tragedy of the commons,' the fishermen of Punta Allen were able to establish a stable and sustainable fishery based on trust, reciprocity, and status. Rules regulating the fishery were developed by co-op fishermen themselves and as such fostered empowerment and a sense of 'ownership' towards proposed enforcement, i.e. fishers recognised that it was in their own interest to respect and enforce regulations. With clear delineation of exclusive zones, fishers could easily detect, and immediately report, whether someone was catching lobster in another fisher's area. The fact that the government respects these regulations and has endorsed them, incorporating them into the Marine Reserve's Management Plan, has served to increase legitimacy of the system. Another important aspect of the process that ensured success was the creation of equitable and efficient marketing strategies, mainly consisting of exporting 30% of the catch alive to Japan, through purposely hired administrative managers. Moreover, the structure in place ensures the sustainability of exploited resources as well as revenues. It also provides a flexible framework that can respond to the demands of the tourism sector, via a system of four cooperative societies for tourist services. Indeed, during the lobster fisheries' closed season (March through June), which corresponds to the peak tourist season, fishers are actively involved in capture-and-release fly-fishing. In addition to taking part in the tourism industry, fishers have been actively involved in research and monitoring aspects of Sian Ka'an fishing activities.

LESSONS LEARNED

Stakeholder Involvement, Empowerment and Community Support

- A sense of ownership of local marine resources should be established, fostering empowerment towards proposed enforcement.

- Trust between community members, reciprocity, and status is essential.

- Clear sentences for those who violate rules should be developed through a consultative process involving all stakeholders.

- Government respect and endorsement of locally drafted regulations is invaluable, increasing the legitimacy of the system.

Zoning and Conflict Resolution

- Zoning can reduce competition between fishers.

- Zoning should be clear, with geographically demarcated lines, as well as clear user rules, facilitating enforcement.

- Low but mandatory resource use fees for participation in a cooperative should be introduced.

Monitoring and Research; Partnerships in Management

- Opportunities to participate in research and monitoring activities; as well as tourism activities during the season closed to fishing, should be created for local stakeholders.

- Creation of equitable and efficient marketing strategies.

Tourism and Sustainable Development

- Flexible frameworks should ensure sustainability of exploited resources and revenues, and be able to respond to the demands of the tourism sector (e.g. system of cooperative societies).

Management Plan of 'Banco Chinchorro' Biosphere Reserve: A Case Study of Concerted Rules and Zoning with Stakeholders

Tomas Camarena Luhrs

Background

The Chinchorro Banc (or Banco Chinchorro Biosphere Reserve (RBBCH)), covering 1,443.60 km², is located in the south-eastern part of the Yucatan peninsula, Mexico, near the border with Belize. The false atoll encompasses a large inner reef lagoon (524.95 km²), four Cays (4.75 km²), and their interior lagoons (1.22 km²) [56], as well as associated unique geological and physiographical reef formations. Declared a Mexican Biosphere Reserve in July 1996 [57], it is being managed by CONANP.[56].

Issues and topics covered

Stakeholder Involvement, Empowerment and Community Support

Partnerships for Management

Monitoring and Research

Zoning and Conflict Resolution

Management Plan Development

Enforcement

Tourism and Sustainable Development

Owing to its relative isolation, the site was visited only by fishermen up until the mid-1980s, at which time recreational divers also, occasionally, began to explore the area. In 1992, the local research institute, Centro de Investigaciones de Quintana Roo, initiated a series of biodiversity monitoring studies and meetings with local fishers who have been using Banco Chinchorro as their primary fishing grounds since the early sixties. Local fisheries mainly target queen conch, lobster (July through February) and scale fish [56]. Fisheries are appointed to three fishing cooperatives (92 members), based in the communities of Xcalak, Mahahual and Chetumal City. Public access to the reserve is permitted occasionally, mainly for scuba diving and snorkelling [56].

When the idea of designating Banco Chinchorro as a MPA was first proposed, fishermen strongly opposed the motion, as they felt it violated their rights as 'owners' of the grounds, despite never having established permanent settlements in the area (principally due to lack of freshwater). As a consequence, implementation of the MPA was delayed until 1996. However, lack of financial support meant that the reserve existed essentially as a paper park up until September 1998, when the government appointed a basic staff of five individuals and allocated basic economic resources to the management of the area.

Monitoring activities were undertaken between 1997 and 1999 by a local NGO, 'Amigos de Sian Ka'an,' with financial support provided by The Nature Conservancy (TNC) and additional support from academic and MPA staff. These activities aimed to establish a baseline for the drafting of a management plan. Work centred on characterising coral-reef habitat, with data collected on abundance and diversity of hard and soft corals (95 recorded species [57]), fishes (over 206 species [57]), sponges, and algae. These data allowed the new managing personnel to start planning a basic zoning system, which was to include 'no take' areas representative of the main ecosystems in the reserve: coral reefs, seagrass (mainly *Thalassia testudinum* [57]), sand beds, and mangroves (*Rhizophora mangle, Laguncularia racemosa, Conocarpus erectus,* and *Avicennia germinans* [57]).

Coverage and health of coral reefs in the Chinchorro Bank Biosphere Reserve. Darker areas represent healthier areas of coral-reef habitat.

Banco Chinchorro is now considered the MPA with the greatest representation of coral reefs in Mexico, both in terms of abundance and health. Moreover, owing to its great biodiversity and the presence of endemic and threatened species (such as marine turtles and a number of reptile and bird species), the National Biodiversity Commission classifies it as a Priority Region A-70, WWF considers it in the global 200 priority areas, and TNC regards it as one of the two priority areas of the Mesoamerican Barrier Reef System [57]. As the largest formation of the MBRS [56], it is also in the process of being included as a World Heritage Site, MAB (Man and the Biosphere) Reserve and as a RAMSAR site.

Description of Activities/Process

In order to ensure compliance with, and support of, any MPA rules and regulations, the reserve's board established a Technical Advisory Committee (TAC) with representation of all stakeholders, including fishers, members of the tourism industry, academic and educational institutions, NGOs, and local, state, and federal governments. The TAC, comprised of 32 Members, met ten times, discussing openly issues pertaining primarily to zoning, prior to reaching full agreement on the management plan. The process was brought to a standstill many times by fishers' leaders who opposed any kind of zoning, as they believed this might lead to the loss of some key fishing grounds. Many of the fishers argued that they could not understand maps, nor figure out the different zone sizes. Therefore, several meetings with the fishers were organized to allow them to visualize each zone's dimensions by demarcating individual sectors using inexpensive buoys. This process was repeated several times until all fishermen showed clear understanding of the discussed regulations, and full agreement was reached amongst all groups.

Results of the monitoring activities, which included over 400 line transects covering the false atoll's 640 km², identified areas with the most diverse and healthy reef habitat. These data, as well as interviews with the fishers, were presented to TAC members for discussion.

Results

Within a year, TAC members reached full agreement on all zoning issues, dividing Banco Chinchorro into areas of no-take, commercial fishing, sport fishing (catch and release only), scuba diving and snorkelling. Full agreement was also reached on a total of 73 rules designed to ensure compliance with, and enforcement of, the reserve. The most significant achievements were: (1) the ban of all fishing activities requiring the use of any type of net, (2) the ban of 'hookah' type air compressors and SCUBA gear for fishing, (3) respect for spawning aggregation sites, and most importantly, (4) the establishment of three 'no-take' areas, defined as 'core zones', covering a total of 45.88 km² (or 7% of the total park area). Moreover, any future tourism development is to be undertaken by, or carried out in cooperation with, the original three fishing cooperatives, based in the communities of Xcalak, Mahahual and Chetumal City [56].

It is important to highlight that the establishment of the TAC, with representatives from all sectors with any interest in the reserve, was key to the development of a flexible and successful management plan (released September 2000)[4]. Nevertheless, enforcement and education need to be improved upon as illegal fishing still poses a serious problem, depleting the resource base for queen conch and lobster [56]. However, it is hoped that an enforcement and surveillance programme, supported by WWF and the reserve, with funds from the Packard Foundation and the Mexican Federal Government, will eliminate such activities and control tourism according to zonation and administrative rules. This programme, making use of two speed boats and an ultra-light airplane, is being developed with the cooperation of legal fishers (who pay 20 cents towards the programme for each kilogram of conch and lobster they catch) and the participation of a number of authorities (Navy Ministry, Ministry of Communication and Transport, and the Ministry of the Environment). In 2001, the Reserve was accorded a GEF (facilitated by the World Bank) patrimonial fund to guarantee the long-term financial sustainability of the park [57].

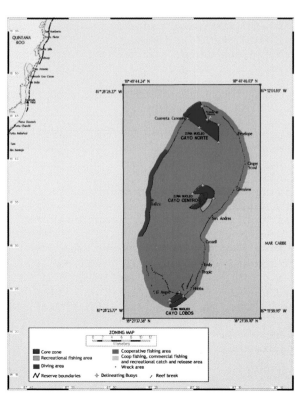

Zonation of the Banco Chinchorro Biosphere Reserve. The red areas highlight core zones, or no-take areas.

---

[4] A digital version of the management plan can be downloaded from the following website: http://www.ine.gob.mx/ueajei/publicaciones/consultaPublicacion.html?id_pub=317&id-tema=4&dir=Consultas

Current Situation

Scientific information on reserve habitats has been significantly improved upon. Universities and research institutions, with the support of reserve staff, have recently produced a comparatively accurate map showing the distribution of individual ecosystems. The GIS is now being updated. This information will be fed into plans for a new zoning scheme, which would increase the size of no-take areas for better representation and management of the reserve. Moreover, there are plans to [56]:

- Integrate and maintain up-to-date databases with all recorded biological, chemical, physical, and socio-economic data.

- Regulate present and future tourist activities, in agreement with the administrative rules of the Management Plan.

- Establish an environmental education programme for all stakeholders.

- Establish an Operative Monitoring Programme for the control and follow-up of socio-economic activities realized in the Reserve.

- Propose and establish a coordination basis with other governmental entities to optimize the Operative Monitoring Programme and management of natural resources.

LESSONS LEARNED

Stakeholder Involvement, Empowerment; Partnerships for Management

- All stakeholders should be actively involved in order to achieve MPA success.

- A Technical Advisory Committee (TAC) should be established, with representatives from all sectors with any interest in the reserve, and often proves key to ensuring compliance with, and support of, MPA rules and regulations.

Monitoring and Research

- Results from monitoring and research are important in helping devise a zoning system.

- Results from monitoring and research can be used to establish a baseline for the drafting of a management plan.

Zoning and Conflict Resolution

- To ensure compliance and enforcement, a clear zoning scheme and clear user rules are necessary.

- The use of non-culture-specific tools (e.g. buoys instead of maps) is important in facilitating common understanding of MPA rules amongst stakeholders.

Management Plan Development

- When designing a management plan, it is important to know and understand the capacities of each stakeholder and adjust development and pace of management plans accordingly.

- Establishment of a TAC, with representatives from all sectors with any interest in the reserve, facilitates the development of a flexible and successful management plan.

Enforcement

- Active involvement of fishers and participation of government authorities in enforcement programmes help ensure sustainability of resource use.

- Enforcement programmes need to be supported by education campaigns.

Tourism and Sustainable Development

- Tourism development is to be undertaken in collaboration with fishers.

Admission Fees: Opportunities and Challenges of Using Admission Fees as a Funding Source at a Small Scale, Tourism Dependant MPA. Case study of the Bonaire National Marine Park, Bonaire

Kalli de Meyer and Fernando Simal

Background

Bonaire, one of the so-called 'ABC' islands (Aruba, Bonaire and Curacao), is situated in the southern Caribbean, approximately 100 km north of Venezuela. It forms part of the Netherlands Antilles, together with Curacao and the windward islands of St Maarten, Saba and St Eustatius. Bonaire is a small, crescent-shaped island approximately 43.5 km long by 8 km wide, with a total land area of 288 km². With a resident population of only 10,000, Bonaire has the lowest population density of any of the Dutch Antilles. The main population centre and tourism development, Kralendijk, is located in the centre of the island, with an older population centre, Rincon, to the north. There are only five other 'villages' and the rest of the island, together with the small satellite island of Klein Bonaire, are both uninhabited and undeveloped. Klein Bonaire, a coral-limestone island located about 750 m off the western shore of Bonaire, possesses active sea-turtle nesting beaches and significant waterbird breeding areas [58].

> ### Issues and topics covered
>
> Stakeholder Involvement, Empowerment and Community Support
>
> Tourism and Sustainable Development
>
> Sustainable Financing
>
> Sustainable Management of Resources
>
> Monitoring and Research
>
> Public Awareness and Education

The islands of Bonaire and Klein Bonaire are surrounded by fringing coral reefs from the shoreline seaward to depths greater than 70 m, covering an estimated 27 km² [58]. Whilst this means that the reefs are very accessible, it also means that they are particularly vulnerable to land-based activities, such as development within the coastal zone. The coastal zone adjacent to Kralendijk has been extensively developed to provide tourist lodging and more recently private residential housing to accommodate an influx of wealthy retirees taking advantage of tax concessions [58]. A sheltered shallow inland bay, Lac Bay, located on the windward shore of Bonaire, represents the largest inland bay in the Netherlands Antilles and is internationally designated as a RAMSAR site. The bay is bounded on its seaward side by exposed fringing coral reefs and supports Bonaire's only significant mangrove and seagrass ecosystems. The mangroves represent an important nesting and roosting area for birds, whilst seagrass beds act as nursery grounds for some species of reef fish and as critical foraging grounds for endangered sea turtles [58]. Given its amazing biodiversity, divers have consistently ranked Bonaire as one of the top ten destinations worldwide, while scientists agree that the reefs themselves are very well developed with exceptionally diverse fish populations.

Moored dive boat on Bonaire. © Kalli di Meyer

Bonaire's economy, like that of many small islands, is remarkably undiversified, consisting of an oil transhipment facility, located on the north-western shore, a solar salt extraction plant, whose condensers take up most of the southern end of the island, and tourism, which is firmly based on dive travel. Dive tourism did not discover Bonaire until 1963, growing from small beginnings – in 1980 there were just four dive operations catering to some 5,000 divers annually – and has now become the mainstay of the island economy. In 1994, an estimated 25,000 divers visited the island, with gross revenues from dive tourism reaching an approximate US$34 million. Currently there are 14 dive operators on Bonaire catering to 25,000-30,000 visiting divers annually. Accompanying Bonaire's diving tourists come an unspecified number of snorkellers, windsurfers, and other water-sports enthusiasts, so that the island now also has two windsurf centres, kayak rentals, parasailing, boating, sailing, and fishing activities on offer to visiting tourists.

The Marine Park

Bonaire has always been very proactive when it comes to conservation. Since 1969 approximately 20% of the total land area of Bonaire has been protected as a National Park. Since 1979, the waters around Bonaire, from the high water mark to the 60 m depth contour, have been designated a marine park, and as such are protected by law. The goal of the Bonaire Marine Park is to protect the island's coral reef, seagrass, and mangrove ecosystems, whilst maximising returns from both recreation and commerce. Activities within the Bonaire Marine Park are therefore regulated in order to ensure the continuing sustainability of the island's marine resources. Destructive practices such as

Bonaire Marine Park dive tag. © Kalli di Meyer

anchoring, coral collecting, and spearfishing have all been banned within the Marine Park for nearly two decades (although there are occasional problems with respect to enforcement of those activities [58]).

The Bonaire Marine Park was first set up in 1979 with grant funding from WWF together with support from the local and Dutch governments. Much was achieved within the park's remit, including the drafting of comprehensive legislation and interpretative information, the establishment of a system of 37 public moorings, and the implementation of research and monitoring programmes. However, after five years, active management ceased and the park became a 'paper park,' existing by law, but with little if any management activity to support it. The fatal flaw for Bonaire, as for many protected areas throughout the world, was the lack of sustainable financial provision for the park once start-up funding had run out. However, sufficient concern was generated for the Bonaire Marine Park to be revitalized in April of 1991. The prime objective during the revitalization process (and one of the conditions linked to the financial support provided by the Dutch overseas aid, Meerjaarenplan Fondsen) was to make the Bonaire Marine Park self-supporting, to guarantee long-term, active management. Administration of the reserve was assigned by the Island Government to Stichting Nationale Parken, Bonaire (STINAPA, Bonaire) under a management contract. The nine-person board of STINAPA represents the park's main stakeholders' interests and has officially appointed representatives from the local agricultural cooperative, fishing community, tourism industry, hotel and tourism association, and dive operators [58]. Whilst the board is responsible for policy decision-making, the park manager is responsible for the day-to-day management of the marine park, finances, and personnel.

In 1999, the marine park area was awarded National Park Status, having complied with the requirements of the Netherlands Antilles Nature Policy plan (i.e. legal protection comprising a sufficiently large representation of local nature and with effective and sustainable management in place) [59].

Diver Admission Fees

To manage the park sustainably, the Island Government of Bonaire decided to introduce a highly controversial annual fee to be levied on SCUBA divers.

A study conducted in 1991 [60] found that 80% of divers were willing to pay a US$20 annual admission fee. However, following exhaustive discussion with all stakeholder groups, the fee was set at US$10 per annum. Despite initial unease on the part of the local dive industry, and threats by highly influential US-based dive magazines to 'boycott' the island, the admission-fee system proved to be successful and found immediate and sincere support amongst visiting divers. Introduced in January 1992, it saw the Marine Park entirely self-supported by the end of the year in terms of its operational costs. Changes were made to the Marine Environment Ordinance (A.B. 1991 Nr.8) to accommodate for the levying of admission fees. It also allowed for one of the most significant precautionary measures to be built into the fee system, namely that, by law, the monies generated may only be used for the upkeep and maintenance of the Bonaire Marine Park, for the provision of education and outreach, the conduct of research and monitoring surveys (e.g. fish censuses, divers impact, CARICOMP and AGRRA related research, coral disease monitoring) and for law enforcement activities.

Divers laying survey transects. © Kalli de Meyer

Moreover, in addition to providing the dive industry and visiting divers with the required assurances to support the fee system, the system has been challenged and upheld by the Island Government. Dive operators administer the collection of the fee on behalf of the Marine Park by making it part of their standard diver check-in procedure. Divers receive uniquely numbered tickets and tags to verify payment of park fees, and are required to display the plastic tag on an item of dive equipment they have with them in the water. Copies of these tickets are returned to the Bonaire Marine Park together with revenues generated on a weekly basis. This way, no overhead or administrative costs are incurred and there is good accountability for the funds.

The admission fee system was conceived as part of a 'total package' to address not only the financial needs of the marine park, but also the need to educate visiting SCUBA divers about the marine environment, and thereby minimize diver impact on the island's reefs. As a result, in addition to the fee payment, dive operators support the reserve by providing:

- Short briefings to all dive guests, during which Bonaire Marine Park rules and regulations are explained.

- Orientation and introductory dives in front of the dive operation to allow operator staff to check that divers have the necessary skills to visit the reef without undue impact.

- Boat briefings to remind and emphasise to divers that they are entering a fragile marine environment where they need to exercise care.

Advantages of the Fee System

In addition to being self-financed, the admission fee system has engendered a number of unanticipated positive 'spin offs' for the marine park. Having paid the admission fee, divers have consistently been keen to receive information on the work and activities of the park, to which the Bonaire Marine Park has responded with outreach materials, brochures, leaflets, posters, and signboards. It has proved surprisingly easy to 'sell' coral-friendly diving ethics to visiting divers, and there has been little or no resistance to compulsory orientations or check-out dives. This may also be due to the fact that the majority of Bonaire's divers come from North America and Europe, where concern for the environment is generally high.

There has been a correspondingly high level of compliance with rules and regulations, even with 'unpopular' ones directly affecting divers such as a ban on disposable glow stick use, and a general prohibition of the use of gloves whilst reef diving.

The level of vested interest amongst divers has been so high that with only five full-time staff to patrol 26 km² of reef, consistent reporting by divers and dive operators has meant that staff are frequently made aware of potentially damaging and illegal activities before they even start. There has also been a high level of support amongst visiting divers for voluntary programmes, such as completing turtle-sighting forms, participating in clean-up dives, or other reef conservation orientated activities.

Disadvantages of the Fee System

Sadly, the biggest problem associated with the diver admission-fee system has been its success, and the ease of payment collection. This has lead to complacency on the part of the management body and stakeholders in general over funding issues. The marine park is currently financially challenged due to a steady increase, over the past eleven years, in the required level of management activity and an accompanying increase in staffing levels. This is coupled with the effects of inflation which have dramatically lowered the purchasing power of the US$10 fees. Additionally, the simplicity of the system has lead to a general unwillingness to consider other viable funding options such as charging for placement or use of piers and private moorings, franchises for businesses operating within the reserve, or exploring other more novel funding solutions. A high degree of dependency on the tourism industry as the major source of funding for the Bonaire Marine Park has also, in some respects, given the industry undue power to veto policy issues with which it does not agree. This is currently reflected in unwillingness on the part of the tourism sector to allow the marine park to raise diver admission fees from their original 1992 level to a more appropriate level, despite proof of divers' willingness to pay US$20 dating back to 1991. Any fee increase is perceived as unfairly 'targeting divers.' At the insistence of the tourism industry, the marine park is now faced with the untenable and un-implementable proposition of attempting to charge all users of the Bonaire Marine Park, including snorkellers, windsurfers, kayakers, boaters, sports fishermen, day charters, parasailers, and water skiers. This is problematic, since all visitors to Bonaire cannot be charged a 'fee' – this would be deemed a 'tax,' and taxes cannot be regulated at the Island Government level. Unlike divers, who require compressed air and therefore access to a filling station, there is no single point of contact for visiting watersports enthusiasts, a significant proportion of whom do not stay at large resort type facilities. This makes both collection and enforcement problematic. Finally, there has always been some resistance to the payment of diver admission-fees by local island residents who consider free SCUBA diving access to the waters around their island a right. So far, this problem has largely been circumvented, as most local islanders who dive work in the dive industry, and their dive operation has traditionally paid their annual admission fee. Given the new proposition, it is once again becoming a controversial subject, as all users are now potentially faced with paying admission fees.

These problems do not currently present easy solutions, given the overarching need and benefit to the Marine Park to continue working in close partnership with the dive and tourism industry. The situation will need to be handled with great care in order to reach an amicable solution.

Material drawn from References [60-70]

LESSONS LEARNED

Stakeholder Involvement, Empowerment and Community Support

- A fee system can lead to complacency by management staff and stakeholders over funding issues.

- Local island residents should be given special consideration when levying fees to access their surrounding waters.

Tourism and Sustainable Development

- A high degree of dependency on the tourism industry as a major source of income can give the industry undue power to veto policies it does not agree with.

Sustainable Financing

- When implementing a fee system to allow for a MPA to be self-sufficient, it is important to think long-term.

- A fee system should be simple to enforce and collection should be easy and regulated.

- Monies levied by a fee system should only be used towards the upkeep and maintenance of a MPA, provision of education and outreach, conduct of research and monitoring surveys, and law enforcement activities.

Public Awareness and Education

- A fee system can have unanticipated positive impacts such as increased interest by tourists in park-related information and high level of compliance and support for volunteering programmes.

Strengthening Relationships: The Case of the Soufriere Marine Management Area (SMMA), Saint Lucia

Dawn Pierre-Nathoniel

Background

Soufriere is a town located along the southwest coast of St Lucia in the Eastern Caribbean [71]. As a volcanic isle with a mountainous interior, the country's population and most of its economic activities are found along a narrow coastal strip. The coastal area, in turn, contains a narrow underwater shelf that supports the island's nearshore fisheries resources. Traditionally and to this day, many households have depended on fishing in the coastal waters of Soufriere as their primary source of income subsistence. Fishers use a variety of technique including pots/traps, lines, seines, and gillnets [72]. Out of an estimated population of 7,665 in Soufriere [73], there are 154 registered fishers (corresponding to 131 fishing vessels) which operate mostly full-time, and land a total of over 80 tons of fish annually [74]. Unlike most fishing communities on the island who target offshore pelagics (e.g. tunas, kingfish, and dolphinfish), Soufriere's fish catch is comprised mainly of coastal pelagics, such as jacks, balao, and sardines, as well as reef species and flying fish.

Issues and topics covered
Stakeholder Involvement, Empowerment and Community Support
Zoning and Conflict Resolution
Development of Management Plans
Tourism and Sustainable Development
Partnerships in Management
Sustainable Management of Resources
Sustainable Financing
Public Awareness and Education

Since the mid-1980s, new tourist-related activities have been increasingly utilising marine resources, competing for access to the area's limited coastal zone [75].

Degradation of coastal water quality, rapid depletion of nearshore resources, poor land use practices and poor resource management, along with growing conflicts among stakeholders, were some of the issues the local government wanted to address through the establishment of a MPA. Disputes often arose mainly between the tourism industry and fishers because of disagreements over use of beaches, anchoring, and responsibility with respect to coral reef damage. Examples of such conflicts and problems are as follows [76-78]:

- Yachtsmen and fishers competed for the use of marine space to engage in mooring and seining activities, respectively.

- There was evidence of indiscriminate anchorage on coral reefs by yachtsmen.

- Community members had conflicts with local hoteliers over access to beach areas for fishing activity (seining) and recreation.

- Fishers had conflicts with the tourism sector and management authorities over the location of a jetty in the Soufriere Bay to facilitate tourism-related traffic; this structure was seen as an obstruction to seining activity.

- Tourism-related vessel operators were accused by fishers of interrupting fishing and damaging fishing gear by passing too close to fishing activity, or directly in the path of deployed fishing gear.

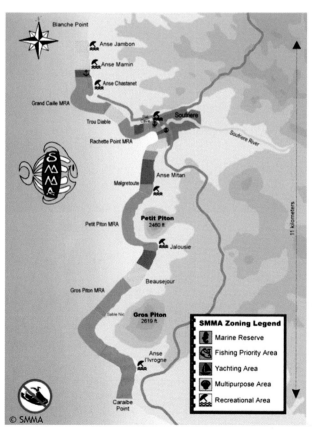

Soufriere Marine Management Area (SMMA), St Lucia.
© *Colette Wabnitz*

- There were problems of visitor harassment by disorganized water-taxi operators offering services to visitors.

- Entry into fragile habitat areas by divers was unregulated.

- Divers were often accused by fishers of deliberately damaging fish pots/traps found during dive expeditions and negatively impacting coral reefs.

- Researchers were accused by fishers of taking fish and coral reef samples, and thus contributing to environmental degradation.

- Uncoordinated and unauthorized marine scientific research was reported to occur.

- The decrease in nearshore fisheries and in the general status of resources was becoming increasingly apparent.

- Degradation of coastal water quality, in particular due to sewage and solid waste accumulation, was a problem with direct ramifications for human health and the integrity of marine ecosystems.

- There was a general lack of awareness of, and appreciation for, the marine environment.

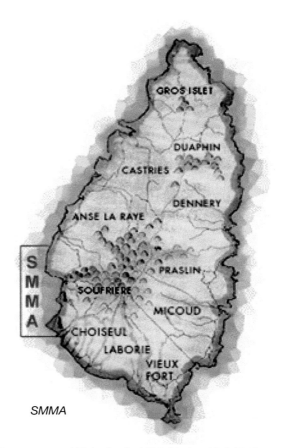

SMMA

The first effort to resolve the situation was led by the Department of Fisheries in 1986. Under this initiative, regulatory mechanisms through the establishment of Marine Reserves (MR) and Fishing Priority Areas (FPA) were developed. However, this initial attempt was largely unsuccessful, due to lack of resources to enforce management, as well as inadequate consideration of, and consequently non-commitment from, local stakeholders. This attempt was followed in 1988 by a more collaborative and participatory process over an 18-month period, initiated through the combined efforts of the Department of Fisheries and two NGOs, the Caribbean Natural Resources Institute (CANARI) and the Soufriere Regional Development Foundation (SRDF). Under this initiative, the coastal zone was surveyed and mapped, and, with the help of resource users, overlain with areas utilized by different groups. This process facilitated discussions aimed at developing a participatory management system [75]. A series of open stakeholder meetings were held with fishers, managers, and representatives from the tourism industry in late 1992 and throughout 1993, and this time key stakeholders reached an agreement on the management objectives for the area [79]. In July 1995, the Soufriere Marine Management Area (SMMA) was officially established (see map for general location of the SMMA).

General location of the SMMA

The SMMA is managed by a non-profit organization, the Soufriere Marine Management Association, which consists of most of the reserve's stakeholders, with technical support from the Department of Fisheries, under the guidance of a Technical Advisory Committee (TAC), comprising key management authorities and user groups [72]. The structure and operation of the TAC indicated the importance of involving resource users in management, as they have the biggest stake in the sustainability of resource use, and an intimate knowledge of the natural resources base [80, 81]. Furthermore, membership and operation centred on co-management as a user-group-centred-approach, without neglecting, nor compromising, the role of government in resource-use management [75]. Increased participation and empowerment at the community level led to an increased sense of ownership and broader park knowledge, which is critical to effective decision-making and sustainability.

Marine Management Area

Following a collaborative and participatory process, an area, stretching 11 km along the coastline, was apportioned into several zones, catering to various uses. The agreed zoning arrangement consisted of [72]:

Zoning of the SMMA

1. *Marine Reserves*: areas considered of high ecological value, closed to any kind of fishing activity, but open to scientific researchers as well as divers and snorkellers by permit only and for a fee.

2. *Fishing Priority Areas*: zones declared for the purpose of maintaining and sustaining fishing activities, which take precedence over any other use of the area.

3. *Multiple Use Areas*: zones where fishing, diving, and snorkelling are allowed under the guidance of existing regulations.

4. *Recreational Areas*: terrestrial (beaches) and marine (swimming and snorkelling) areas, which are reserved for public access and recreation.

5. *Mooring Areas*: sites for visiting yachts and recreational boats. A coral conservation fee is charged for the use of the moorings.

Since the SMMA was formed, and through the combined efforts of resource users, management authorities, scientists, non-governmental groups, donor organizations, and the Soufriere community, numerous achievements have been made. They can be summarized as follows [75, 76, 82-85]:

- Reduction or resolution of conflicts among users, through a consultative and participatory process, and through improvements in communication between these groups, researchers, and management agencies. This has led to better coexistence of users in a shared coastal zone, and increased commitment to the conservation, sustainable use, and equitable sharing of benefits from resources.

- Collaborative management of the area, through the formation of a multi-sectoral, multi-disciplinary TAC, comprising government organizations, NGOs, community members, and resource users. This has helped to increase a sense of ownership for the SMMA initiative, through the direct involvement of resource users in management, and has provided a forum for open and continuous dialogue.

- Increased awareness about environmental issues.

- Generation of user fees, which has essentially led to self-sufficient financing of the SMMA.

- Provision of a valuable area for scientific study for researchers.

- Improvement in the status of coral reefs, especially branching coral [86], which had previously been subjected to physical damage, particularly from anchorage.

- Increase of fish stocks in marine reserves and fishing priority areas [86], also reflected in an increase in fishers' catches [87].

However, the road to success was not an easy one. In the early stages, despite some immediate achievements, several hurdles had to be overcome prior to achieving true support for the SMMA. Fishers reported that they were experiencing declines in fish catches and blamed the SMMA for promises of increases that never occurred. While it was unrealistic to expect significant results in fishing priority areas within a few years of marine reserve implementation, and notwithstanding habitat destruction and high sedimentation in the Soufriere coastal zone from unnaturally heavy rain in 1995 and 1996, the disillusionment of the fishers cannot be understated. This situation was amplified by the feelings of fishers that the 'rich,' predominantly white tourists that visit the SMMA, and the local restaurateurs, hoteliers, taxi operators (water and land-based), dive operators, charter boat companies, and sightseeing operations, were the only parties benefiting from the SMMA arrangement. In the fishers' view, their livelihoods were being compromised. The lack of vision, the failure to finalize a 'draft management plan,' the inadequate legal/enforcement regime, the initial institutional/representation deficiencies among the TAC, and the lack of resources may have contributed substantially to the disagreements and misunderstandings amongst stakeholders. Participation and collaboration, which form the heart of the SMMA, began malfunctioning and decisions were increasingly taken by small groups of people outside the TAC, without the joint negotiation and consensus process agreed to in the original documents. These decisions included, for example, the negotiation by small groups for the extension of a fishing priority area, which led to encroachment on a marine reserve, the access by select fishers to specific sections of two marine reserve areas, and the sharing of part of a fishing priority area with yachtsmen. As a result, fishers started infringing upon SMMA regulations by placing their fishing gear within marine reserves. Inadequate resources, both human and financial, as well as the lack of a clear and effective enforcement regime, exacerbated local conditions. The situation culminated in serious threats made to the SMMA manager, brought on in part by displaced workers who turned to fisheries as an alternative source of income, increasing tension, and a change in government, which encouraged fishers to advocate for change on all fronts. In an effort to address these issues, the TAC began an intense consultative and participatory review of the SMMA, highlighting its strengths and weaknesses and making recommendations towards improved management. This led to the formulation of a more efficient and effective SMMA management structure. Under the new Agreement (see Table), an eleven-member Board of Directors was established.

The 'Agreement to Manage the SMMA' [88] was officially signed by the partners in January 2001 and a president 'with proven knowledge and experience in the field of development and management' [89] was appointed for a renewable period of two years. The new structure, with its associated Agreement and Bylaw, *inter alia*:

The new institutional arrangements for the management of the SMMA

LESSONS LEARNED

Stakeholder Involvement, Empowerment and Community Support
- Increased participation and empowerment at the community level leads to an increased sense of ownership, recognition, and improved park knowledge, critical to effective decision-making and sustainability.
- International recognition of conservation efforts leads to increased popularity and pride.
- In order to avoid non-compliance with MPA rules, care should be taken to include adjacent communities which may use the MPA.
- Clear and open communication mechanisms increase stakeholders' commitments to conservation, sustainable use, and equitable sharing of profits; breakdown in communication may lead to conflicts and non-cooperation.
- The establishment of a TAC comprising key management authorities and user groups is important in addressing stakeholders' needs and implementing a MPA that will be accepted and enforced.

Development of Management Plans
- When implementing a MPA, its vision and mission need to be clearly identified and the role of all contractual parties clearly defined.
- Regular reviews of a reserve's management plan, highlighting its strengths and weaknesses, can help in the formulation of a more efficient and effective management structure.
- Management plan structures should give a MPA a strong legal basis.
- Lack of vision and failure to finalise draft management plans can contribute to disagreements and/or misunderstandings amongst stakeholders.

Tourism and Sustainable Development; Partnerships in Management
- When establishing partnerships between the public and private sector, a formal agreement should be outlined and clear role sharing should be defined.
- Development of a co-management system should neither neglect nor compromise the role of government in resource management.
- When developing tourism activities, it is important to ensure that profits are being shared equitably.

- Provides a clear vision and purpose;

- Gives the SMMA a stronger legal basis;

- Provides the SMMA with more autonomy;

- Clearly defines the roles of all contractual parties;

- Elucidates a process for review and evaluation;

- Is binding upon all partners; and

- Improves the partnership between the public and private sectors though formal agreement and clearer role-sharing.

Efforts were also made by the government of St Lucia, through the Department of Fisheries and the SMMA, and with the assistance from donor organizations, to alleviate some of the socio-economic difficulties faced by Soufriere, largely caused by loss of fishing grounds through the implementation of the SMMA. Such initiatives included the construction of a jetty, the introduction of Fish Aggregating Devices (FADs), training in the use of longlines, the establishment of an investment fund, the construction of a fish market, and the provision of an ice machine. Moreover, under the new arrangement, the SMMA had a clear mission, namely: 'to contribute to national and local development, particularly in the fisheries and tourism sectors, through the management of the Soufriere coastal zone, based on the principles of sustainable use, cooperation among resource users, institutional collaboration, active and enlightened local participation, and equitable sharing of benefits and responsibilities among stakeholders' [71, 72, 88].

The SMMA has been internationally recognised for its conservation efforts, and awards have included the 1997 British Airways Tourism for Tomorrow; IUCN Special Award for National Parks and Protected Areas; and a position in the top five along with Algeria, USA, Spain, and Canada for the 1997 World Underwater Confederation (CMAS) International Marine Environmental Award (GPIEM). The SMMA has also been a popular model as a 'lessons learned' case study at local, regional (Caribbean region), and international levels.

LESSONS LEARNED

Stakeholder Involvement, Empowerment and Community Support

- Increased participation and empowerment at the community level leads to an increased sense of ownership, recognition, and improved park knowledge, critical to effective decision-making and sustainability.

- International recognition of conservation efforts leads to increased popularity and pride.

- In order to avoid non-compliance with MPA rules, care should be taken to include adjacent communities which may use the MPA.

- Clear and open communication mechanisms increase stakeholders' commitments to conservation, sustainable use, and equitable sharing of profits; breakdown in communication may lead to conflicts and non-cooperation.

- The establishment of a TAC comprising key management authorities and user groups is important in addressing stakeholders' needs and implementing a MPA that will be accepted and enforced.

Development of Management Plans

- When implementing a MPA, its vision and mission need to be clearly identified and the role of all contractual parties clearly defined.

- Regular reviews of a reserve's management plan, highlighting its strengths and weaknesses, can help in the formulation of a more efficient and effective management structure.

continued...

...continued

- Management plan structures should give a MPA a strong legal basis.

- Lack of vision and failure to finalize draft management plans can contribute to disagreements and/or misunderstandings amongst stakeholders.

Tourism and Sustainable Development; Partnerships in Management

- When establishing partnerships between the public and private sector, a formal agreement should be outlined and clear role sharing should be defined.

- Development of a co-management system should neither neglect nor compromise the role of government in resource management.

- When developing tourism activities, it is important to ensure that profits are being shared equitably.

Zoning and Conflict Resolution

- To be effective and ensure reduction/resolution of conflicts, MPA boundaries should be geographically well demarcated and user rules well-defined and enforced, with appropriate penalties for offenders.

- A zoned MPA provides a valuable area for scientific study for researchers, i.e. No take = controls; and fishing priority zones = reliable data.

- Zoning represents a management tool through which multiple uses are supported, and conservation as well as sustainable utilization of resources made more compatible.

Enforcement

- Powers of arrest granted to rangers can enable them to carry out their duties more effectively.

- Inadequate legislative basis for the management and regulation of MPA may lead to the development of problems and conflicts.

- Lack of an effective regime for enforcement of user fees can exacerbate conditions should conflicts arise.

Sustainable Financing

- User-fee systems can lead to self-sufficient financing of a MPA, if:

  - Revenues are clearly earmarked for conservation and park management activities.

  - Payments are simple to enforce and collection easily regulated.

Sustainable Management of Resources

- Sustainable management of marine resources requires the implementation of effective regulations *on land* concerning issues such as coastal development, land use, and waste disposal.

- Successful management results in the improvement of substrate health and increases in fish stocks inside and outside of a MPA, as well as increases in fishers' catches.

Public Awareness and Education; Capacity Building

- Awareness-raising and education activities are essential for MPA recognition and acceptance.

- Governmental organizations, non-governmental groups, and the media can help raise awareness by involving and sensitising fishers to the work of researchers.

- Capacity building of uncoordinated water-taxi operators, and the implementation of Water Taxi Association, can lead to more viable business and reduced visitor harassment.

Community Policing and the 'Culture of System-Beating': The Honorary Game Wardens and Fisheries Inspectors of the Portland Bight Protected Area (PBPA), Jamaica, West Indies

Peter Espeut

Background

Portland Bight was declared a protected area in April 1999. It is Jamaica's largest protected area covering 1,876 km², of which 520 km² are terrestrial and 1,356 km² marine, encompassing 47.6% of Jamaica's shallow shelf [90]. At least 19 residential communities are located directly on the coast, contributing to a population of over 50,000 inhabitants [91].

The MPA is home to a wide diversity of wildlife, both native and migrant. Portland Bight has the largest remaining mangrove system in Jamaica, which, together with extensive seagrass beds, provide probably the largest nursery area for fish, crustaceans, and molluscs on the island [92]. The protected area also harbours extensive coral reefs associated with 16 coral cays [90]. The mangrove system is under serious threat, as many residents derive their livelihoods from cutting mangrove poles and forest trees to produce charcoal and to use for timber, fuelwood, fenceposts, stakes, and local products [91]. Snorkelling assessments of the reefs indicated that some reefs are being heavily impacted by land-based nutrient pollution (mainly arising from lack of proper sanitation, sewage disposal facilities, solid waste disposal, and chemical effluent) and sedimentation (due to unsustainable land-use planning), and suffer from the lack of herbivorous fish (mainly due to over-fishing) and urchins, whilst others are in reasonably good condition [92]. Reefs closest to Kingston Harbour and the Rio Cobre River appear to suffer particularly high algal growth rates [90]. With the exception of Port Royal, little is known about reefs off the south coast, where distance from shore limits accessibility. Off-shore cays and banks such as the Morant Cays and Pedro Bank are even less accessible [90].

> ### Issues and topics covered
>
> Stakeholder Involvement, Empowerment and Community Support
>
> Partnerships for Management
>
> Development of Management Plans
>
> Enforcement
>
> Sustainable Management of Resources
>
> Public Awareness and Education

Management objectives of the park are to achieve (1) sustainable use of natural resources, (2) improve the quality of life of local residents, (3) protect threatened species (e.g., turtles, crocodiles, and manatees) and ecosystems (e.g., seagrass, mangrove, and coral reef), (4) involve communities in the planning, monitoring, and enforcement activities of the Portland Bight Protected Area (PBPA), (5) increase environmental awareness, (6) establish financial sustainability, and (7) develop efficient and effective community capacity [93].

Resource Management – the Jamaican Context

Efforts to conserve the natural environment often fail, even where there is adequate environmental legislation, due to non-compliance with these regulations, and the high cost of enforcement. Non-compliance may have a variety of causes: financial gain, lack of environmental awareness, a don't-care attitude towards the environment, lack of an alternative, damaging behaviour being cheaper or easier than environmentally-friendly behaviour, and the absence of deterrents due to the lack of enforcement. Each of these problems requires a different approach. Whilst natural-resource managers must be flexible enough to deal with a suite of varied problems, they must also design programmes to raise environmental awareness, set up motivation initiatives, and give advice regarding alternative technologies and income sources. In less developed countries where the rate of population expansion often exceeds that of job openings, and poverty frequently drives people to unsustainably exploit natural resources, enforcement of compliance must be done sensitively, and must not appear to be repressive. However, it must also be sure to serve as a deterrent (which is a compliance strategy in itself) and visibly identify, apprehend, and prosecute offenders. The environmental degradation and lack of compliance with environment regulations for which Jamaica is famous has taken place in the context of the traditional top-down approach to management used in the last few centuries. In order to fully understand the failure of such a system to successfully and sustainably control natural resource exploitation, it has to be placed within Jamaica's historical context.

Jamaica was a slave society before 1834, where societal order was maintained by the local militia raised by the plantation owners and their white staff. Jamaica's police force was reformed in 1865 after a major rebellion by former slaves. Their grievances centred principally on inequality in the justice system: judges, prosecutors, and juries were all recruited among plantation owners – their former slave masters - and consequently former slaves hardly ever won a case in court. The plantation owners controlled the formal economy, and to protect their labour supply severely constrained the options for social and economic advancement for the vast majority of Jamaicans (disempowerment). In the reforms which followed, a professional magistracy was created (a positive move), but the constabulary force established was basically at hand to protect the privileged. Distrust of the police and a desire to 'beat the system,' perceived to be unjust, part of the cultural ethic of working-class Jamaicans. Stories about the escapades of the Jamaican folk hero 'Anancy' (who migrated to Jamaica with Akan-speaking slaves from the area now known as Ghana) describes a survivor who avoids direct confrontation, but beats the system through slyness, deceit, and trickery. In this context, this 'culture of system beating' is found in Jamaica at all levels, even among those whose ancestors mostly hail from Europe rather than Africa. Thus, the challenge of natural resource management lies not just in dealing with ecological issues, but also in facing the often-made, but often-ignored, point that natural resource management is more of a social science than a natural science.

The 'Culture of System-Beating' and Development of a Sense of Ownership

The 'culture of system beating' can be defined as people seeking to defeat a regulatory system that belongs to somebody else, operates in someone else's interest, or is perceived to do so. However, should a system of laws and regulations operate or be perceived to operate in one's own interest, compliance may reasonably be expected to increase. Hence, the first strategy towards increased compliance is to create within the users of local natural resources a sense of ownership.

For fisheries management within the PBPA, this was done in the following ways:

- At each of the six fish-landing sites within the Protected Area, fishers, vendors, scalers, repairers, etc. were encouraged to form a fisheries association/cooperative.

- For each association, a seminar was conducted where stakeholders themselves identified problems facing the resources their fisheries depend upon, and possible solutions. These were remarkably similar to fisheries management strategies drawn up by fisheries biologists, but since the fishers identified the list of problems and solutions themselves, they 'owned' the list.

- Delegates from each association and from relevant government agencies were assisted to establish the 'Portland Bight Fisheries Management Council' (PBFMC), a genuine stakeholder council. The PBFMC (including government delegates) collated the management suggestions from each association into a suite of fisheries management regulations with assigned penalties for infringement of regulations.

- This set of rules and regulations was sent to each of the fishers associations for ratification or amendment. Meetings were held on each beach to allow discussion of individual policies until full agreement was reached. Following some modifications, a final set of fisheries management regulations was drafted.

- This final draft was formally sent to the Ministry of the Environment (a member of the PBFMC), which sent them on to the Office of the Chief Parliamentary Counsel (OCPC) for final writing into law.

- The version from the OCPC was reviewed article by article at the annual Portland Bight Fisheries Conference held on International Fishers Day (June 29), and approved.

PBPA survey sites. Source: PBPA

- These laws are now awaiting ratification by the Minister of the Environment.

At the end of the outlined process, the fishers' organizations and their individual members felt they 'owned' the set of laws, as opposed to having regulations imposed from higher levels. Thus, stakeholders are avid advocates for their promulgation and enforcement.

However, there were two weaknesses in the process: (1) not all fishers were members of the fishery associations at the landing sites, and (2) not all members, and non-members, attended the beach meetings. Nevertheless, given that the vast majority of fishers supported the fisheries management regulations, potential errant fishing activities (by the individuals belonging to the categories above) are likely to be controlled and justly punished, should they arise.

Community 'Honorary Game Wardens' and 'Fishery Inspectors'

Even when a local community owns regulations controlling its fishery, individuals may still resent outsiders coming in and arresting their relatives and friends for non-compliance. To avoid such a situation, community leaders are to be appointed as enforcement officers. By means of a provision of the Wildlife Protection Act and the Fishing Industry Act, about 50 fishers were officially appointed 'Honorary Game Wardens' and 'Fishery Inspectors' by Jamaica's Head of State, the Governor-General. These Acts convey powers of arrest (without warrant if the enforcement officer witnesses the offence) and powers of search, without warrant, of any vessel the enforcement officer believes has been used to commit an offence, or contains a catch obtained illegally. It also authorizes the enforcement officer to impound any vessel if any evidence is found. Such empowerment of community leaders reinforces their personal and community authority, and strengthens the effectiveness of the fisheries organizations themselves.

Each year, the Caribbean Coastal Area Management Foundation (C-CAM) provides three days of training to all Honorary Game Wardens and Fishery Inspectors in the provisions of the laws they enforce and in the mechanics of making an arrest; cautioning the accused (the Jamaican equivalent of 'being read your rights'); taking a statement; preserving evidence; and testifying in court. It is made clear to the trainees that the objective is compliance, not making arrests, and numerous warnings have been given to encourage future adherence to the laws and regulations. A significant concern associated with such an approach is that community Honorary Game Wardens and Fishery Inspectors might abuse their authority. Careful selection of suitable individuals, thorough training, and close supervision by C-CAM have resulted in no known abuse of authority or false arrest since 1996, and a 100% conviction rate in those cases which have gone to court. Another worry has been that community Honorary Game Wardens and Fishery Inspectors would 'excuse' their friends and relatives, and harass their foes, or take bribes. This issue is also addressed during training, and no such case has been reported. On the contrary, interestingly, it has been found that community Honorary Game Wardens and Fishery Inspectors advise their relatives and friends not to embarrass them by committing an offence, as they would be obliged to personally arrest them to prove they are not corrupt. This proves to be particularly true for female Honorary Game Wardens and Fishery Inspectors who have warned their partners, sons, sons-in-law, and nephews. Finally, it must be pointed out that firm enforcement cannot be done by these community volunteers alone. Some have been threatened with bodily harm (e.g. by dynamiters), and they have been advised to make full reports of all observations to C-CAM and take no further action. No Honorary Game Warden or Fishery Inspector is expected to put his/her life in danger – also, at the moment, none of them is insured. Once regulations have officially been made into law, the protected area will benefit from full-time Protected Area Rangers will full police powers hired by C-CAM who will follow up on the intelligence provided by local community members.

In many parts of the world, getting communities to police themselves is being encouraged. The approach being taken in the PBPA is a version of this, and should advance the discourse. This approach has the potential to be effective for other types of offences such as traffic violations, breaches of health, and planning regulations. Its implementation has been straight-applied sociology, confirming the point that 'fisheries management is not the management of fish; it is the management of the activities of people.'

LESSONS LEARNED

Stakeholder Involvement, Empowerment and Community Support

- Creating a sense of ownership of laws and regulations within users of natural resources can increase compliance; feeling as owners, community members are then avid advocates for their promulgation and enforcement, leading to successful and sustainable management of resources.

- Establishment of a fishing cooperative and stakeholder council can be crucial to creating a sense of ownership within users of natural resources.

- Granting community leaders powers of arrest and search reinforces their authority and strengthens the effectiveness of the fisheries organizations.

- Non-members of fishery associations, and individuals who did not attend participatory meetings and discussions about management plan development, are the ones most likely to breach policies.

- When the vast majority of community members support management regulations, it is likely that they will apply peer pressure to 'defecting' individuals.

- An adequate legislative basis for the management of a MPA fosters community support.

Development of Management Plans

- When developing a management plan, a true collaborative and participatory process of designing, assessing, and revising sets of guidelines should ensure wide ranging support of the drafted regulations, as well as their effective enforcement.

Partnerships for Management

- Endorsement of park management regulations by local government officials is important to increase legitimacy of drafted rules.

Enforcement

- Enforcement must make sure to act as a deterrent and visibly identify, apprehend, and prosecute offenders.

- Initiatives where communities police themselves should be encouraged.

- Enforcement of compliance with regulations should be done sensitively.

- Responsible and non-corrupt community members should be assigned as enforcement officers to justly punish offenders.

- Adequate training of Honorary Game Wardens and Fishery Inspectors in the provisions of the laws can lead to proper enforcement of regulations.

- Firm enforcement requires support by individuals with full police powers.

Sustainable Management of Resources

- When regulations lead to improvement in habitat health and visible increases in fish stocks, sustainability of successes registered in participatory processes will be ensured.

Public Awareness and Education

- Environmental-awareness-raising activities should be an integral part of MPA management.

Conflict Resolution between Inter-Sectoral Stakeholders for the Buccoo Reef Marine Park Coastal Zone in Tobago: The Pigeon Point Case Study

Arthur Potts

Background

Buccoo Reef Marine Park (BRMP) is located on the southwest coast of Tobago, a 300 km² island in the Eastern Caribbean made up of jungle-covered hills at its centre, fertile soils on its plains, and a variety of sandy beaches. Originally part of the South American continent, Tobago has retained many of the flora and fauna of South America [94]. The park itself consists of the Buccoo Reef and the Bon Accord Lagoon Complex. Covering a marine area of 1.5 km² and a terrestrial area of 3 km² the MPA comprises a reef system protecting an extensive shallow lagoon bordered by a fringing mangrove forest [95]. As Tobago's most popular attraction, the area's

> **Issues and topics covered**
>
> Stakeholder Involvement, Empowerment and Community Support
>
> Development of Management Plans
>
> Tourism and Sustainable Development
>
> Zoning and Conflict Resolution
>
> Sustainable Financing

marine and coastal resources are being used intensively for tourism and other commercial and/or subsistence purposes. As a result, major resource conflicts are being played out along Tobago's coastal margins [95].

At the request of the Tobago House of Assembly (THA), the Institute of Marine Affairs (IMA) carried out ecological studies of a number of reefs around Tobago (including Buccoo) between 1984 and 1985. Based on these surveys, water quality measures, socio-economic studies, public education and awareness, as well as legislative evaluations, the Management Plan for the Buccoo Reef Marine Park was completed in January 1995. It addressed such issues as management structure, legislative changes, surveillance, park-boundary demarcation and zoning of uses, moorings installation, monitoring, pollution control, licensing of park visitor users fees, public education, and interpretative facilities. Also included was an assessment of the park's financial viability. Within its limited scope, the analysis produced a negative assessment, but subsequent analysis based on a willingness-to-pay survey produced a positive assessment of viability. After 18 months, the THA officially accepted the document and agreed to implement its recommendations in June 1995 [94]. These included issues of access, surveillance, and enforcement, safety requirements and equipment, pollution control and management control. However, in addition to financial and human capacity constraints, implementation and enforcement of BRMP regulations and recommendations have not been adequate [94].

In the meantime, the development of the commercial fishing industry in Tobago is running ahead of the state's efforts to put in place necessary physical infrastructure and support services that must complement private sector entrepreneurship and investment if the industry is to survive and prosper. Awaiting the implementation of the government's plans to provide them with beach facilities and accesses, fishers have erected small buildings as close as possible to the sea. Boats are moored nearby at historic landing sites around the island's coast, and thus fishers use the BRMP primarily as a launching and landing site. Recently, due to tourism-related developments, both government and private tourism developers are contesting the use of many of these sites by fishers, reef tour operators, and others operating in Buccoo Reef Marine Park Area. Fishers and other stakeholders are being asked to move (or are being moved) in order to allow for tourism development plans to proceed. Fishers, in particular, believe this to be both unfair and unjust, and have expressed their desire to cooperate in jointly deriving a plan that would allow them to share the waterfront. They are now calling for urgent government intervention (both at the local and national levels) to provide security of tenure for their beach sheds until the promised public facilities are built and made available to them. They also contend that, as part of the right to carry on utilising seafront space, they should also have the right of free public access to these sites. Fishers have expressed confidence in the government's ability to resolve this conflict, and have pointed to the Three Chains (Tobago) Act as a useful reference.

The following is a brief account regarding the historical context within which to place access to Pigeon Point (the southernmost point of Buccoo Reef) and the present impasse regarding the use of Wind Hole, Pigeon Point.

Pigeon Point Access Point

For a number of years, the lands surrounding Pigeon Point were owned by *Gordon Grant Investment Company*. During those times, for the most part, fishers were allowed free access to their boats, day or night, located at Wind Hole, the safest anchorage point on the whole island at the back of Pigeon Point. In the mid-eighties, *Amar* leased the land at Pigeon Point from *Gordon Grant Investment Company*, and established a truce between fishers and the management of the facilities: fishermen were allowed access through the gates and to the beach at all times. In the early 1990s, a new lease contract was signed between the *Ansa McAl Group of Companies* and *Gordon Grant Investment Company*. Initially, fishers retained free access rights to the beach, but occasional conflicts between stakeholders arose, mainly due to (failed) yearly efforts from *Ansa McAl* to get fishers to pay an entrance fee to access beach property. Following *Ansa McAl*'s purchase of land at Pigeon Point in 1996, the new management decided that the area should be administered as Club Pigeon Point Beach Resort, and the property was registered as a private club. In 1997, the new owners attempted to destroy the established fishing shacks on the beach, which resulted in a lawsuit that is still before the courts.

In February 2000, the management of Club Pigeon Point Beach Resort instituted a charge to fishers as an entrance fee to the beach. Access times through the gates were to be between the hours of 0800 and 1900. These rules were arrived at by the resort's management alone, without any consultation, participation, or agreement process being instigated with fishers and/or other stakeholders. This led fishers to stage a protest at the resort's gates on 8th March 2000 (Ash Wednesday, one of the busiest days of the year), preventing anyone from accessing the beach. Both the Director and Secretary of the Department of Marine Resources and Fisheries intervened, and the protest was called off about midday. Plans were also made at that time for conflicting parties to discuss the matter, and for a meeting between all stakeholders to be chaired by the Director Marine Resources and Fisheries, Tobago House of Assembly (THA), with a view to reaching an amicable solution.

At the meeting three critical conflict issues were identified:

1. Entrance fees.

2. Time of access to and from the beach through the gates.

3. The use of Resort Identification cards by fishers to access Pigeon Point.

It was agreed that a second meeting, hosting the same participants, should be convened on 20 March 2000. At this second meeting, it was agreed that fishermen would not be charged an entrance fee, and that they would be allowed access through the gates between the hours of 0500 and 2100 daily. However, no agreement was reached on the pass/ID issue. The owners of the Resort insisted on the use of their Club's Passes only, while the fishermen contended that they should be allowed to use their Fisherman's IDs. The management of the Resort thus decided to allow fishers to use their IDs until both parties would revisit the matter in June 2000. The Department of Marine Resources and Fisheries chaired a number of meetings with relevant stakeholders, and in the end fishers agreed to the use of a Club pass.

Despite active efforts by the government and the implementation of internationally-funded collaborative projects aimed at fostering community awareness and stakeholder involvement [96] over a number of years, many of the issues regarding the use of the Pigeon Point marine area by fishers and other sea-front stakeholders still need to be resolved. In addition, new conflicts are arising as a result of planned tourism development; although fishermen have been assured by the state that they will benefit from the development of new facilities along the beach.

LESSONS LEARNED

Stakeholder Involvement, Empowerment and Community Support

- Without public consultation and involvement, MPA regulations are likely to be inappropriate or redundant for reasonable use by stakeholders.

- External stakeholders who have a stake in a MPA and have influence should also be included in consensus-oriented meetings/workshops.

- Staging of meetings is a useful and important tool for consulting and engaging local stakeholders in any decision process that affects any one group or all groups.

- Meetings and conflict resolution processes should be driven by local community participants.

- In order for projects to be successfully implemented and compromise to be reached, community groups should, from the onset, define a clear mission and definite goals.

- When setting up collaborative projects, partners should communicate openly and be clear on, and agree on, the objectives of given activities.

Tourism and Sustainable Development

- If revenues generated by tourism development, which impacts areas utilized by all stakeholders, are not shared equitably, conflicts are likely to arise.

Zoning and Conflict Resolution

- Conflicts between stakeholders are likely to arise when there are no clear rules or zoning for temporal and spatial use of resources, due to a lack of understanding of each others' needs and priorities.

Sustainable Financing

- Unless a MPA is financially self-supporting in the long-term, it is unlikely to be effective.

PART VI
THE EAST AFRICAN REGION

The Eastern African Region is composed of Somalia, Kenya, Tanzania, and Mozambique on the African mainland continent, and the islands of Comoros, Madagascar, Mauritius, Seychelles, and La Reunion (France).

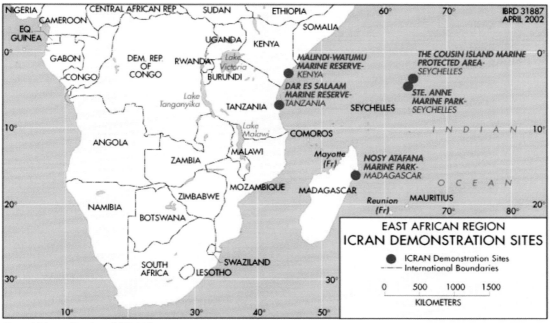

East African Region (ICRAN)

The Region – Habitat, Population, and Economic Characteristics

The region's marine environment is characterized by patches of mangroves, coral reefs, seagrass beds, large estuaries, sandy beaches, cliffs, and muddy tidal flats [97]. The coast of mainland East Africa harbours an almost continuous string of coral reefs from Somalia to the northernmost region of South Africa, with warmer temperatures in the central region and cooler areas off the coast of Somalia and South Africa. The extensive fringing, barrier, or platform reefs are only broken by major rivers, carrying large nutrient and sediment loads and thus restricting coral reef growth in those areas [98]. Around island states, reefs vary from fringing (Comoros, Madagascar, Mauritius, Reunion and Seychelles), to isolated atolls (Comoros, Seychelles and Mauritius), and large submerged banks. A significant proportion of local communities are highly dependent on marine and coastal resources for their livelihoods, through both artisanal and commercial reef related fisheries, as well tourism (over two million travellers visit the region annually, bringing in about US$1 billion [99]). In addition, the reef structure provides considerable protection from large ocean swells and strong cyclonic activity [100].

Over 17 million people live along the Eastern African coast (30 to 35 million people if one includes the island states, corresponding to 60% of the region's population [99]) and tend to be clustered around the main cities (e.g. Mombasa, Dar es Salaam). The rapid rate of human population growth and widespread poverty, particularly in coastal areas, is straining both resources and educational facilities. The growing number of coastal fishermen, primarily as a result of

Fishing boat in Bazaruto Archipelago, Mozambique. © Colette Wabnitz

49

the perceived economic opportunities, has led to increased pressure being applied on to the marine and coastal resource base and resulted in declining catches [99], putting the fishermen themselves at risk of losing their jobs, and increasing conflicts among stakeholders [101].

Over-exploitation of natural resources (mainly of small fish, octopus, shellfish, sea cucumber, and lobster), destructive fishing practices (e.g. dynamite, pull-seine nets, poisons, and dragnets [102]), and coral bleaching events are the main threats to coral reef biodiversity. Industrial and domestic pollution, lack of treatment facilities for sewage disposal, coral mining for lime making, sand mining for construction purposes (particularly in Mauritius and Comoros [100]), deforestation, poor land-use practices (e.g. deforestation, agriculture, and coastal construction), which contribute to increased runoff and siltation, as well as poorly managed and unplanned tourism have also significantly contributed to reef decline. With rapidly expanding population centres, threats to reefs are only likely to further increase, and as a consequence, the stability of local, national, and regional economies, as well as people's existence, are at stake [99]. Tourism has been a great contributor to this problem. Although it is a major component of the economy of the region's countries, its expansion has often taken place in the absence of necessary environmental assessments, resulting in net income losses for the region, partly due to ecological degradation (e.g. Kenya has suffered a 40% drop in revenue) [99].

Coral bleaching and mortality during the 1998 El Niño event impacted all reefs in the region, with the most severe damage recorded in Seychelles, Comoros, and particularly Tanzania and Kenya, where mortality levels ranged between 50% and 90%. In contrast, corals in Madagascar, Mauritius, and La Reunion suffered less severe bleaching and recovered relatively quickly. Recovery at severely impacted sites has since been patchy [103], with higher recovery rates generally being recorded on inaccessible reefs and inside MPAs (e.g. Chumbe Island, Mombasa Marine Park), with the exception of a few cases such as Malindi Marine Park [104]. Reefs closest to population centres exhibited significant decline in coral cover, in particular in Madagascar, and to a lesser extent Comoros. Massive floods in southern Mozambique in 2000 reduced live coral cover even further [105] (60% to 95% decline in the Xai Xai lagoon) due to sedimentation. In addition, Harmful Algal Blooms (HAB) and a fungal disease caused high mortality in various coral species on many reefs in Kenya and Tanzania. Recent incidences of bleaching have been reported in 2003 for reefs in Tanzania, Kenya, and the Seychelles [106].

Management

The socio-economic importance of reefs to the region's communities, in particular to artisanal and small scale fishing, is receiving increased attention, partly due to the severe coral loss incurred during the 1998 bleaching event [98].

Artisanal small scale fisher in Mozambique.
© Colette Wabnitz

Furthermore, monitoring activities in the region involving community members (especially in Tanzania) have come to play an increasingly important role in projects aimed at establishing and managing MPAs. Indeed, following the 1998 bleaching event, East African countries have demonstrated increased efforts at cooperating to improve regional consistency of monitoring data and reporting, through networks of scientists, managers, and policy makers, both at national and international levels. In late 2001, through the Nairobi Convention, an intergovernmental task force on coral reefs was established by Eastern African nations (including islands) in an effort to strengthen and stimulate regional coordination, support, and monitoring for coral reefs. In addition, the countries have implemented measures to reduce fishing pressures and are increasingly devolving power to local communities to monitor and manage their own marine and coastal resources, for the most part, facilitated by conservation and community development initiatives [100].

In the context of Integrated Coastal Zone Management (ICZM), often put forward as the best framework to address the array of issues facing the coastal zones, MPAs are being used in the region as a tool to help combat over-fishing, promote sustainable development, and protect valuable habitats and associated species [97]. Lack of adequate institutional arrangements has represented the greatest constraint to the successful implementation of ICZM [99]. Although it is recognised that research and monitoring of coral reefs and their resources are important for generating management information, most reef areas (including MPAs) do not have consistent and continuous programmes [103]. However, recent developments at the local level to enhance institutional arrangements and the increased level of local and international support accorded to governments and communities (mainly by NGOs and tourist operators) in the region have proven valuable. With the guidance of the Indian Ocean Commission, a regional monitoring network was formed in 1998 to assist island nations in managing their reef resources. This network functions as a GCRMN node. Through funding provided over a three-year period by the GEF (administered by the World Bank) and the European Union (EU), new initiatives are building on existing ones and strengthening national monitoring capacity [13].

Assessments have shown that, on the mainland, a fair number of MPAs have been managed relatively effectively, with most countries seeking to create new MPAs and improve upon the management of existing ones. Lessons learned in park management have been widely shared and plans are in progress to create a network of cross-boundary marine reserves along the coastline. In late 2003, following the declaration by South Africa to create new MPAs, the government of Mozambique announced its immediate intention to protect the important Zambezi Delta, a 6,700 km^2 zone that includes the second most important mangrove system on the East African coast. The Minister of Tourism also announced Mozambique's commitment to establishing new MPAs in the northern coastal provinces of Nampula and Cabo Delgado, as well as the southern coastal province of Maputo. Both South Africa and Mozambique also pledged their support to establish a transboundary marine protected area from the Maputo Special Reserve in Mozambique, down to the Greater St. Lucia Wetlands Park, South Africa [107].

Limiting factors in management and enforcement success of existing MPAs have been the reticence of fishermen to accept full no-take zones and the lack of sustainable financial support and capacity. The latter issue is being targeted by several training initiatives and development of MPA manager networks to enhance cooperation and sharing of information, incorporating indigenous knowledge and using local expertise. Moreover, a great number of national and international NGOs (e.g., IUCN – the World Conservation Union, WWF, ICRAN, UNEP, and the Western Indian Ocean Marine Science Association (WIOMSA)) have been collaboratively implementing a number of activities to assess and improve the understanding of effective MPA management and develop tools to achieve this. For example, WWF East Africa has been conducting a series of consultative workshops with the goal to establish a regional network of MPAs and corridors. ICRAN, implemented through UNEP, is developing projects focusing on the management activities exhibited at two sites, the Malindi-Watamu MPA complex and Dar es Salaam Marine Reserves [98]

In contrast, few MPAs have been established in the southwest Indian Ocean region, and existing monitoring stations lack sustainable funding, capacity, and enforcement of regulations in place. However, a number of international NGOs (e.g. Conservation International (CI) in Madagascar, Shoals of Capricorn, Rodrigues) are setting up meetings and developing targets to strengthen national coastal development policy, in addition to training and monitoring activities (e.g. GEF-funded Seychelles Marine Ecosystem Management Project, GEF/EU funded Indian Ocean Commission programme). In addition, the Coral Reef Degradation in the Indian Ocean programme (CORDIO) is assessing ecological as well as socio-economic impacts of bleaching in the region with the financial support of the World Bank, the Swedish Development Agency (SIDA), other governments, and WWF. ICRAN has been supporting local community involvement in the design of effective management principles for MPAs in Chumbe Island (Tanzania), the Nosy Atafana Marine Park (Madagascar), The Cousin Island Marine Protected Area (Seychelles), and Ste Anne Marine Park (Seychelles) [100].

Regional Seas Programme of East Africa

In 1996, the Eastern African states adopted a Regional Convention for the Protection, Management, and Development of their Marine and Coastal Environment, which led to the establishment of the Eastern African Regional Coordinating Unit (EAF/RCU) in Seychelles. Its mission is 'to provide leadership and encourage partnerships by inspiring, informing, and enabling nations and people of the Eastern African Region and their partners to protect, manage, and develop their Marine and Coastal Resources in a sustainable manner.'[108]

As the Secretariat, it is responsible to the Conference of the Parties and intergovernmental meetings, comprising Comoros, France, Kenya, Madagascar, Mauritius, Mozambique, Seychelles, Somalia, United Republic of Tanzania, and most recently South Africa. It also administers the Action Plan of the Nairobi Convention, including the Protocol Concerning Protected Areas and Wild Fauna and Flora in the Eastern African Region; and the Protocol Concerning Cooperation in Combating Marine Pollution in Cases of Emergency in the Eastern African Region [109]. Moreover, the EAF/RCU implements ICRAN activities within the region.

CASE STUDIES

Implementing ICRAN Activities at the Malindi/Watamu MPA Complex Demonstration Site, Kenya

Nyawira Muthiga and Robert Njue

Background

The Malindi-Watamu National Park and Reserve, formally declared in 1969 [97] and designated as a MAB reserve in 1979, was designed primarily to conserve some of the country's reefs [97]. Covering 213 km², it is located about 100 km north of Mombasa and stretches for 30 km along the Kenyan coast [110]. Its jurisdiction extends five kilometres from the coast and includes beaches situated just south of Malindi town and areas beyond the entrance to Mida Creek, a large, almost land-locked expanse of saline water, characterized by mangrove forest and inter-tidal mudflats protected in the Watamu Marine Reserve. The Malindi-Watamu reserve also features rock platforms, cliffs, sandy beaches, coral reefs, and sea-grass beds [110]. There are important turtle nesting sites within the reserve, and a number of marine mammal species have been reported within the boundaries of the MPA. The park itself is characterized by a buffer zone referred to as marine reserve, where traditional forms of fishing are permitted [97].

Issues and topics covered
Stakeholder Involvement, Empowerment and Community Support
Partnerships for Management
Zoning and Conflict Resolution
Capacity Building
Socio-economic Issues
Public Awareness and Education
Sustainable Management of Resources
Monitoring and Research

The Malindi-Watamu Marine Protected Area complex project was initiated by the Kenya Wildlife Service (KWS) and UNEP as one of the activities of ICRAN in Kenya. The project area comprises the Malindi Marine Park and Reserve and the Watamu Marine Park and Reserve, including Mida creek. Although the adjacent Arabuko Sokoke forest is not strictly in the project area, the important ecological linkages between Mida Creek and the forest make Arabuko Sokoke an area of concern. The project is managed by KWS Coast Regional Headquarters through the Coastal and Wetlands office, whilst MPA offices coordinate the day-to-day implementation activities of the project. Staff include a warden as well as rangers and other assisting staff (e.g. SCUBA rangers, security rangers, and gate rangers who collect revenue) [111]. The Coastal and Wetlands Office currently implements many projects with similar and related objectives including management planning, research, monitoring, and awareness and capacity building for the wise use and management of wetlands. Fees from all National Parks and Reserves are managed by KWS and re-distributed from the central budget to protected areas around the country [104].

The main objectives of the project include:

- The preparation of a detailed profile for the demonstration and implementation of management action strategies for the MPA complex.

- The development of small-scale infrastructure to enhance the management of the MPA complex.

- A review of social, cultural, and poverty alleviation issues, in order to develop a better understanding of the stakeholder issues.

- A review of current management plans.

- The development of a training and education network through the Malindi Resource and Training Centre.

As this area is an important recreational centre in Kenya, local communities benefit from tourism activities through boat trips, water sports, and deep sea fishing [110]. Threats to local reefs and mangroves include over-exploitation of marine resources such as finfish and invertebrates. Increasing siltation from the Sabaki River and mortality due to bleaching constitute other important threats to the reserve's reefs [110].

Capacity for MPA management in the Park is developing, and ICRAN assistance has been directed towards supporting a number of activities including:

- Capacity building for MPA management.

- Development of training manuals.

- Community-based management plans for boat operators associations and code of conduct.

- Upgrade of Malindi and Watamu Boat Operators offices, boats and engines, insurance, and snorkel equipment.

- Targeted research in MPAs, including reef and mangrove restoration, impacts of users, and stock assessment.

- Training for Malindi and Watamu boat operator's associations in visitor-handling and business-management techniques.

- A regional management-effectiveness initiative in collaboration with IUCN.

Several institutions — KWS, The Wildlife Conservation Society (WCS), and CORDIO — are involved in ecological monitoring activities, which involve the annual collection of information on benthic cover, coral and fish diversity, coral recruitment, and fish abundance [104]. Increasing dialogue between collaborating institutions, the local administration, fisher communities, the tourism sector, and local residents has led to the re-examination and adaptation of a draft management plan that includes socio-economic information.

Financial support to date has been provided by KWS/Netherlands Wetlands Conservation and Training Programme (training, moorings, management plans, buildings, visitor centre, boats, and other marine equipment), the Coral Reef Conservation Project (CRCP) (biophysical monitoring), Kenya Marine and Fisheries Research Institute (KMFRI), Moi University, and other international universities (research) [111].

WATAMU - MALINDI NATIONAL PARK AND RESERVE

Consultative meeting of Malindi Boat Operators Association to discuss ICRAN activities.
© Kenya Wildlife Service

Activities and Progress

PREPARATORY MEETINGS

The project was introduced to all relevant stakeholders including MPA boat operators, residents living adjacent to the MPA, communities fishing in the marine reserve, and hotels on beaches adjacent to the MPA. In addition, consultative meetings were held with the Malindi and Watamu Boat Operators Associations, the Watamu Conservation group (members include residents, businesses, and hotels in Watamu), Arabuko Sokoke Management Committee, and A Rocha Kenya (an NGO that is working with local communities in Mida creek). The project was also introduced to, and endorsed by,

53

the District Development Committee. This not only served to raise awareness about ICRAN in the Malindi/Watamu area, but also helped create an atmosphere of cooperation and ownership that was crucial to the smooth implementation of the project.

PLANNING MEETINGS

The planning meetings were held between the Wardens and the KWS Coast Regional Headquarters to discuss accounting and reporting requirements of the project. Moreover, the amount of support required from KWS Coast office and the development of a monitoring mechanism were also reviewed. A workplan was then developed detailing the various steps and expected outputs of the project as well as monitoring indicators.

The Wardens indicated that the ICRAN project had received much publicity and that there were high expectations by local communities. Hence, it was decided that high-profile activities should be undertaken at the beginning to build on the momentum and interest generated in the preparatory meetings.

Progress

OBJECTIVE 1: PROFILING INFORMATION

The Malindi Warden attended a MPA management effectiveness workshop organized by IUCN and WIOMSA in Zanzibar. Skills learned and developed during this workshop have greatly enhanced the ability of the administration to appreciate and utilize appropriate management information.

Currently, conflict data, maintenance data, visitor statistics, reserve fisheries catch data, and biophysical data have been compiled for both MPAs. In addition, a small library has been established in the resource and training centre and many reprints and publications have been acquired from the coastal library. A bibliographic library database has also been developed. The Malindi MPA now has an internet connection that is reasonably consistent. Although telephone contact in the Watamu office is now reliable, the lack of a computer has considerably slowed down electronic communication. However, at the time of printing a second computer and accessories has been donated through ICRAN to the Malindi-Watamu MPAs complex, facilitating further courses at the Resource and Training Centre, and management of the park in general.

A team of scientists from CRCP, KWS, and Moi University were commissioned to produce a biophysical profile; a draft is available and is currently under review.

OBJECTIVE 2: SMALL-SCALE INFRASTRUCTURE DEVELOPMENT

All the construction works in the MPAs have been satisfactorily completed. In addition, rehabilitation of the Malindi boat operators' offices and shop, not initially planned, was also completed.

A review of the monitoring equipment currently housed in the MPAs was carried out and additional diving and snorkel equipment purchased for both Malindi and Watamu Reserves. Repairs of Park boats and engines have also been completed. Regular mooring maintenance and water quality monitoring exercises have been implemented after training by KMFRI, with funding from the KWS/Netherlands Wetlands Conservation and Training Programme.

OBJECTIVE 3: SOCIO-ECONOMIC ISSUES

Support to target communities included expansion of the Malindi boat association engine storage facility and repair of their offices and community shop. The handing over ceremony was conducted by the member of parliament for the area. In addition, the Malindi boat repair workshop has been restored and will be available for use by local boats, thereby greatly reducing costs for storage and repair at the current boat yard in Malindi. In Watamu, the engine room was constructed below the Watamu boat operators' association office.

The socio-economic assessment of Malindi's boat operators highlighted gaps

Ceremony to hand-over the Community Boat Engine Storage Facility presided by the Malindi Member of Parliament. © Kenya Wildlife Service

The awareness building (bottom left, middle top), education, and outreach materials and programmes at the Malindi visitor centre. © Kenya Wildlife Service

in the capacity of the boat operators in business management and investment. These findings will be used to support development of a proposal to be submitted to the UNDP Small Grants Program (UNDP SGP). The bird-hide for the community boardwalk was completed and has become an integral part of the overall ecotourism project, Arabuko-Sokoke Schools & Eco-Tourism Scheme (ASSETS), which A Rocha Kenya is implementing at Mida Creek and Arabuko-Sokoke Forest. The bird hide and boardwalk through the mangroves at Mida Creek, together with interpretative displays, will improve the quality of the visitor experience and ensure sustainable use of the creek and forest through effective management of visitor activities. Financial benefits from the facilities (100% of fees from their use) flow directly back into the local community in the form of bursaries for children's secondary school tuitions. The location of the bird hide is near the neap high-tide roost of up to 5,000 migrant waders and flamingos.

OBJECTIVE 4. AWARENESS AND EDUCATION

Awareness equipment including TVs, VCRs, tapes, and brochures have been purchased and installed at the Malindi Visitor Centre as well as the Watamu awareness hut. Regular records of school visits indicate that approximately 120 schools, tertiary institutions, and Universities visit Malindi every year, making the visitor centre a reliable venue for dissemination of awareness information.

Challenges and Opportunities

At the beginning, lack of understanding about the project among target communities presented an obstacle. This was mainly due to the high expectation created after news about large sums of funds allocated to ICRAN. The Malindi Fishermen's Cooperative Chairman met with KWS and indicated he would not support the project if funds were not directly disbursed to the community. A number of meetings were then organized to clear up the misunderstanding. Communities in the project area are now sufficiently aware of project objectives and its mode of implementation.

There are many areas that still require support, but ones in need of immediate attention include:

- The Watamu park base is poorly equipped for communication as well as for monitoring activities. Lack of a computer and an office space has greatly constrained the ability of the management staff to run scientific and awareness activities, compared to the capabilities of the Malindi park base.

- Despite repair and rehabilitation of boats and engines, the latter require a great deal of high-cost maintenance. Their replacement is crucial to guarantee the continuation of key activities in the MPAs, including those pertaining to monitoring, surveillance, and safety.

- The Mida-Creek community boardwalk needs more support to ensure visitor safety. It also requires an expansion to enable the generation of additional revenue for adjacent communities.

- Evaluation of training needs and implementation of targeted training of local community boat operators would greatly enhance their ability to conduct their businesses.

Despite the above-listed challenges, this project has generated a number of useful lessons relating to the implementation of community projects at this ICRAN site. Specifically, the project has served to enhance the partnership between local communities and managers, as a consultative process was applied throughout the implementation phase. The focus on management effectiveness has generated momentum within KWS, and most MPA managers are now embarking on collection of information for the initial assessment of MPAs. Under the Jakarta Mandate project, implemented by IUCN-Regional Office for East Africa (IUCN-EARO), ICRAN has provided funding for a management effectiveness assessment initiative, and a workshop that was held in Malindi (2003). Further opportunities to develop other projects exist, for instance through the UNDP Small Grants Programme (SGP). An initial visit by UNDP has led to discussions about developing a proposal for a community-based initiative involving Malindi boat operators. In addition, the KWS/Netherlands Wetlands Conservation and Training Programme has indicated an interest in providing further support for the development of the Malindi Resource and Training Centre. Reef Check, an ICRAN partner, carried out a pilot training programme in June 2003, with the aim of perhaps developing a regional Reef Check training node based at the Malindi centre.

The Centre also acted as the field site for the East African Wetlands Management Course conducted by the KWS Training Institute in October, 2002. This opportunity was brought about thanks to the rehabilitation and upgrade of available accommodation, the improved training centre, and other MPA facilities. It is hoped that the Malindi centre will serve as a hub for training in coastal and wetlands programmes in the future (the Regional MPA managers training course is scheduled to be held at the training centre in September 2004).

Implemented activities have been favourably reviewed during site visits by the Director and Assistant Director of KWS, Mr. R. Hepworth (Deputy Director, Division of Environmental Conventions, UNEP) and Dixon Waruinge (Coordinator of the Nairobi Convention, UNEP), Dr. C. Gakahu and Dr. Esther Mwangi (UNDP-SGP), the District Officer Malindi, the Chiefs and MPs of the area. To date, the achievements of the project continue to be highlighted as a success story at important regional and international meetings, including the Regional ICRI meeting in Mexico (2002), the first Coral Reef Task Force Meeting and Group of Experts in MPA (GEMPA) meeting organized by WIOMSA, as well as the WSSD meeting in South Africa, thereby increasing opportunities for networking and collaboration with other regional programmes. Moreover, a recently published study [112] on the effects of marine reef National Parks on fishery Catch Per Unit Effort (CPUE) has demonstrated that for most species, CPUE in traditional 'Dema' traps fished across park boundaries was higher, by up to an order of magnitude, within parks than outside of MPA boundaries. The study further concluded that although spill-over of most species from the reserves is limited, the most important commercial species exhibit significant spill-over from adjacent fisheries. Finally, the MPAS are likely to represent important nursery and growth areas for other species [112].

Material drawn from References [113-115]

Reef Check training programme participants in front of boatshed. © Neville Ash

LESSONS LEARNED

Stakeholder Involvement, Empowerment and Community Support

- Without clear communication between all stakeholders, misunderstandings can arise, creating confusion, lack of trust, and delay in implementation of regulations.

- Successful achievements and management effectiveness will result in increased recognition and the development of opportunities, particularly regarding networking and collaboration.

- A focus on management effectiveness can generate momentum amongst managers and managing bodies.

Partnerships for Management

- The establishment of a consultative process enhances partnerships between local community members and managers.

- Endorsement of regulations and attendance at official events by government officials increases the legitimacy of management actions.

Capacity Building; Public Awareness and Education

- Capacity building is required to increase management effectiveness.

- Basic infrastructure is required to allow for management to be carried out effectively.

- Training of park wardens can greatly enhance the ability of administration to utilize and appreciate appropriate management information.

- Evaluation of training needs and implementation of targeted training of local community boat operators can greatly enhance their ability to conduct their businesses

Monitoring and Research; Alternative Livelihoods and Socio-economic Issues

- Socio-economic information, in addition to ecological data, should be incorporated into a management plan.

- Specific biophysical targets should be incorporated into management plans.

Sustainable Financing

- Lack of long-term financial support can severely and significantly limit MPA effectiveness.

Monitoring and Research

- Biological and socio-economic monitoring and research represent important components of successful MPA management.

Challenges and Opportunities of Managing Marine Reserves Surrounded by Poor Population and Urban Settings. Case study of the Dar es Salaam Marine Reserves System, Tanzania.

Amin Abdallah and C.K. Rumisha

Background

The Dar es Salaam Marine Reserves System (DMRS) was established under fisheries legislation in 1970 and gazetted in June 1975. It was transferred to Marine Parks and Reserves in 1998 with the aim to foster the area's aesthetic, recreational, educational, and research value [116] as well as facilitate sustainable utilization of natural resources in specified areas [102]. Its Board of Trustees is the custodian and overseer of the establishment and management of the Marine Protected Reserves in Tanzania [116]. The park itself is located to the north of the city's main harbour entrance on a shallow continental shelf, and comprises a system of four marine reserves, mainly small islands (Fungu Yasini, Mbudya, Pangavini and Bongoyo) and their surrounding waters [102]. These marine parks include coral reefs, mangroves, and seagrass beds [98] hosting high levels of biodiversity.

The islands of Mbudya, Pangavini, and Bongoyo are coral islands, with an area of 0.53 km^2, 874 m^2, and 0.81 km^2, respectively. While Mbudya and Bongoyo islands host sandy beaches, Pangavini Island is surrounded by steep cliffs, making it inaccessible to humans. The coastline along the reserve is characterized by extensive expanses of sand, with small patches of mangroves at Kunduchi and Tegeta river mouths, and a much larger mangrove stand at Ras Kiromoni. The intertidal zone is very extensive around the reserves and dominated in its lower sandy parts by seagrass, but includes rock and sand, as well as encrusting and soft corals. Lower intertidal and subtidal areas are characterized by some coral cover [102].

However, due to the park's proximity to Dar es Salaam, with a population of around three million, these fragile ecosystems are coming under increasing pressure from national and local economic development. Many of the local communities living in Kunduchi, Unonio, and Msasani, adjacent to DMRS, are poor, subsisting on less than US$1 a day, and depending entirely on marine resources for their livelihoods [117]. These local communities, together with fishers living in neighbouring villages and from localities further along the coast, come to the DMRS area to take advantage of the relatively abundant marine and coastal resources and the proximity to markets. However, while coral reef monitoring surveys in the 1960s and 70s reported

> ### Issues and topics covered
>
> Stakeholder Involvement, Empowerment and Community Support
>
> Tourism and Sustainable Development
>
> Partnerships for Management
>
> Alternative livelihoods and Socio-economic Issues
>
> Zoning and Conflict Resolution
>
> Enforcement and Compliance
>
> Sustainable Management of Resources
>
> Public Awareness and Education
>
> Sustainable Financing
>
> Monitoring and Research

Patrol Boat, Tanzania. © Eastern African Coastal and Marine Environment Resources Database and Atlas (EAF/14 Project).

high diversity of corals and associated species, censuses carried out in the 80s and 90s described a general degradation of coral reef ecosystems, associated with declines in biodiversity, mainly due to increasing fishing pressure exerted on the reserves' system, in conjunction with the use of destructive fishing practices (e.g. drag nets, dynamite, and beach seining [118]) [102]. Fishermen have been complaining about declines in fish catches, which they also attribute to the use of destructive fishing practices, mainly small mesh nets (beach seine in particular)

Fishermen, Tanzania. © Eastern African Coastal and Marine Environment Resources Database and Atlas (EAF/14 Project).

and dynamite fishing [116]. Other threats include land reclamation, sand mining, and coral mining for construction purposes; collection of marine organisms for the curio trade [118]; lack of industrial and domestic effluent treatment; unsustainable shipping activities; oil pollution; and dredging of the harbour mouth, resulting in increased sedimentation and hence smothering of surrounding coral reefs. In addition, increased wastewater and sewage discharge have reduced water quality, and anchor damage is visible throughout the reserve. Lack of trained personnel and resources to enforce legislation have also contributed towards coral reef degradation [102].

The DMRS also faces the displacement of poor community residents to the suburbs of residential areas, mostly further away from beaches, potentially preventing access to resources they depend upon for subsistence. Many of the problems associated with environmental degradation centre on poverty as both a cause and effect [117]. District fisheries statistics document a decline in the number of fishermen in Kunduchi and Msasani over the last ten years, with only a total of 823 fishermen operating from these two villages, compared to 1443 in 1989 [118]. Rapid unregulated tourism development has led to numerous hotels being built with diving facilities right on the shoreline. Resources-use conflicts have arisen between tourist and local fishers, as access to beaches and landing sites have been denied to fishers, whilst fishers complain that anchor damage from diving boats is significantly contributing to the decline in health of the region's coral reefs. Tourists, on the other hand, complain that fishing activities have led to severe declines in fish stocks and the transformation of reefs into 'graveyards.' This situation is exacerbated by the fact that fishermen and tourists have been using the same sites, namely those areas of highest fish abundance, thus bringing both groups into direct contact and/or conflict [118].

With ICRAN's support, the DMRS management has succeeded in capitalizing on these challenges and turning them into opportunities by effectively, actively, and positively engaging all relevant stakeholders (e.g. local fisher communities and private sectors) to support the effective management of the reserve. Examples of successfully implemented activities include:

- Environmental education and awareness raising.

- Applying the lessons learned at DMRS by trying to develop an effective national network of MPAs in Tanzania.

- Development of a General Management Plan (GMP) that aims to build on these experiences to ensure the sustainable utilization of DMRS resources.

Opportunities for DMRS

The proximity of the DMRS to Dar es Salaam, and thus influx into the park system of both local and foreign visitors, has allowed the reserves' management, together with the private sector, to develop and implement a financial framework for the conservation of the park's resources through the collection of visitors' as well as business concession fees. The public-private partnership, established through the fee-collection mechanism, has brought about positive attitude changes amongst all stakeholders towards building mutual trust and open support to the reserves. This mutual trust has further strengthened the participation and involvement of the private sector, both in the management of DMRS as well as in support regarding equipment and ideas. Furthermore, the park is strategically located to allow for regular field trips (e.g. schools, businesses, and public at large) and has developed effective environmental education and awareness campaigns.

Through ICRAN funding, honorary park rangers (for the most part former 'beach boys') have received training in tourist guiding as well as monitoring of local resources. In addition to assisting in the management duties of the reserve, such as patrolling the reserve; reporting on illegal activities; checking entry permits; monitoring sea-turtle nesting activities; coral-reef monitoring and coral transplantation; they participate in diving activities and act as taxi-boat drivers, thus diversifying, and thereby increasing, their sources of revenue. They also make tourists feel safer, contributing to a more positive image of the reserves. These successes have been registered in the increase in number of visitors from 4,000 (in 2000) to 10,000 in two years. Increases in live coral cover [119] and the active promotion of the reserves through the Marine Parks and Reserves Unit, in collaboration with tour operators and hotels, may also have contributed to this success. It is hoped that through greater involvement of local communities in management decisions, improved enforcement of regular patrols, and development of public-private sector partnerships, management costs of the reserves will be reduced, allowing for the long-term conservation and financial sustainability of the DMRS to be ensured.

DMRS, with ICRAN's support, is currently in the process of developing a GMP to effectively involve all stakeholders and ensure the sustainable utilization of DMRS resources. ICRAN is also providing support to [116]:

- Improve existing infrastructure, such as the installation of buoys to delineate boundaries and the establishment of a visitors' centre.

- Provide training for communities and rangers, including guide training and boat engine maintenance [116].

- Awareness raising initiatives, including the provision of information products [116].

- Target communities, including the construction of a community mangrove boardwalk and a boat repair facility [116].

- Conduct biophysical and socio-economic studies.

The Way Forward

Although successes have been registered mainly through increased environmental awareness, an appropriate management structure to protect the environment and its resources is still missing. Plans to increase park effectiveness include:

- Changing DMRS status from Marine Reserve to Marine Park, leading to a multi-user system within a framework of ICM for the Dar es Salaam coastal area [116].

- Finalising the GMP, which benefits from the overwhelming support among all user groups, building on lessons learned to ensure sustainable resource use. A considerable amount of information is available on the biological riches of DMRS, though several areas still require consideration.

- Developing a plan for fishing area and seasonal closures [116].

- Enforcing MPA regulations through the establishment of regular patrols [116].

- Installing additional mooring buoys in sites receiving large numbers of visitors, i.e. Bongoyo and Mbudya.

- Continuing to work with partners such as ICRAN, IUCN, WWF, Tanzania Coastal Management Partnership (TCMP), local communities, private sectors, and other local initiatives to ensure effective management of existing MPAs and encourage the implementation of others.

- Linking with other ICRAN sites and other MPAs in order to share experiences and transfer knowledge.

- Building capacity amongst local communities to further support MPA management processes and comprehensive programmes aimed at raising further awareness of conservation and management issues.

- Developing a comprehensive and regular programme of ecological monitoring including intertidal resources, seagrass beds (which are more likely to sustain the DMRS fisheries than coral reefs [102]), coral reefs and mangroves, as well as fisheries data [98]. Such monitoring activities should adopt a constant study methodology at carefully selected sites in order to allow for data comparisons over time and space.

Material drawn from References [120, 121]

LESSONS LEARNED

Stakeholder Involvement, Empowerment and Community Support

- Engaging local communities as well as the private sector in all management decisions is crucial to support development of trust among stakeholders.

- Development of trust among stakeholders is key to effective management of a reserve, as well as subsequent enforcement of its regulations.

- Building capacity amongst local communities and training members to work within MPAs, provides alternative incomes and increases support for MPAs significantly.

Tourism and Sustainable Development

- Park rangers should be allowed to engage in tourism related activities, in a regulated manner.

- Dissemination of information and promotion of a reserve through government institutions and tour operators can help contribute to greater visitor numbers, as well as a more positive image of a reserve.

Partnerships for Management

- Good partnerships between public, private sector, and local communities can be a powerful tool in capitalizing on challenges and turning them into opportunities.

- By engaging all stakeholders in management decisions, effectiveness of a reserve can show considerable improvement.

Alternative livelihoods and Socio-economic issues

- The socio-economic aspects of a reserve, in addition to ecological data, need to be incorporated into a management plan

Zoning and Conflict Resolution

- The establishment of a zoning scheme is a useful tool to promote conservation of biological resources.

- Zoning provides for a variety of sustainable uses, whilst minimising conflict between user groups.

- Different use areas should be clearly demarcated.

Enforcement and Compliance

- Enforcement is essential to warrant sustainable use of resources and conflict resolution.

continued...

...continued

Public Awareness and Education; Capacity Building

- Through adequate training, former 'beach boys' can be turned into Honorary Park Rangers.

- Awareness-raising and education campaigns, as well as capacity building are important aspects of MPA management.

- Proximity to a large city can be capitalized on through the development of effective environmental education and awareness campaigns.

- Large numbers of visitors, especially from local origins, allow for opportunities to develop effective management education and awareness campaigns.

- Sharing of experiences between sites is an important experience and a useful tool to disseminate lessons learned.

- By building capacity amongst local communities, support for MPA management can be significantly fostered.

Sustainable Financing

- Levying of visitor and business concession fees can allow for the development of a financial framework supporting the conservation of the park's resources.

- Through greater community involvement, improved enforcement, and development of public-private sector partnerships, management costs of a reserve can be reduced.

Monitoring and Research

- A management plan should incorporate a regular programme for the monitoring of ecological and fisheries data that make use of a standard methodology, so as to allow for comparisons over time and space.

PART VII
The East Asian Seas Region

The Region – Habitat, Population, and Economic Characteristics

In addition to hosting 34% of the world's coral reefs, covering approximately 100,000 km², and encompassing the world's highest coral diversity, Southeast Asia also contains over 61,000 km² of mangroves, representing approximately 35% of the world's total [7].

East Asian Seas region (ICRAN).

With 350 million people living within 50 km of the coast, communities in Southeast Asia are heavily reliant on marine and coastal resources for their livelihoods. This is particularly true of small-scale fishermen living in rural areas and relying, at times solely, on these resources both as a source of income and for food [7].

In the last 50 years, Southeast Asia has experienced rapid industrialization and population expansion. Human population growth has been associated with increases in pressures on natural ecosystems at unsustainable rates, ranking coral reefs of Southeast Asia as the most threatened in the world. However, over-exploitation of resources has not only occurred because of increased local consumption [122]. It has also been associated with the development of trade in live reef food fish and marine ornamentals, often using destructive capture techniques such as blast and cyanide fishing [122]. Many of the region's reefs have already been severely damaged. A recent study estimated that about 88% of the region's reefs were at risk, with about 50% suffering from high to very high stress levels [7] (see figure, top of page 64). Overfishing (64% of reefs), destructive fishing practices (over 56% of coral reefs), unplanned and poorly managed coastal development, improper land use and deforestation, dredging; mining of sand and coral, sewage discharge, and pollution, represent the main threats to reef ecosystems [7]. Reefs in the Philippines, Vietnam, Singapore, Cambodia, Taiwan, and China constitute some of the most threatened in the region [7]. In addition to anthropogenic impacts, reefs in Indonesia (particularly along the northern coast of Java (Ketut Sarjana Putra pers. comm.) and the Philippines have suffered moderate to low mortality rates due to the 1998 bleaching event, whilst reefs in Thailand suffered high losses in live coral cover (up to 80-90% in certain areas).

Fishers in Thailand. © David Gandy

63

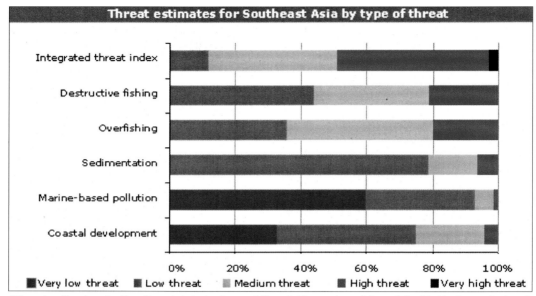

Threat estimates for Southeast Asia by type of threat. Reproduced from [7] with kind permission from the lead author.

Tourism is growing rapidly in Southeast Asia, and in many countries throughout the region it provides an important incentive for coral-reef conservation. Many small-scale or traditional fisheries are progressively being replaced by tourism. When managed sustainably, healthy reefs located in areas with good tourism potential can provide an estimated US$700 to US$111,000 per km² in annual revenues (Table 4). Tourism can also benefit communities not directly involved in tourism business by providing local populations with alternative livelihoods, reducing fishing pressure and alleviating poverty [7]. Unfortunately, lack of effective and proper planning, as well as lack of effective management schemes for sustainable tourism [11], have resulted in development that negatively affects reefs (Table 4).

Although the region displays numerous MPAs, they only cover 8% of its reefs and, for the vast majority, are poorly and ineffectively managed (38% have inadequate and 48% partially effective management) [7]. Thus, in actual fact, just 1% of the region's reefs are in MPAs considered to be effectively managed. Lack of finances, lack of local community participation, low capacity for monitoring, and unsuccessful enforcement are the main setbacks to successful management in the region [7]. However, international NGOs are increasingly focusing attention on the region in an attempt to reverse environmental degradation,

Table 4 – Potential sustainable annual economic net benefits (per km²) of healthy coral reef in Southeast Asia. Reproduced from [7] with kind permission from the lead author

Resource Use (direct and indirect)	Production Range	Potential Annual Net Benefits (US$)
Sustainable fisheries (local consumption)	10 – 30 tonnes	$12,000 – 36,000
Sustainable fisheries (live fish export)	0.5 – 1 tonnes	$2,500 – $5,000
Coastal protection (erosion prevention)		$5,500 – 110,000
Tourism and recreation	100 – 1000 persons	$700 – $111,000
Aesthetic/biodiversity value (willingness-to-pay)	600 – 2000 persons	$2,400 – $8,000
Total (fisheries and coastal protection only)		$20,000 – $151,000
Total (including tourism potential and aesthetic value)		**$23,100 – $270,000**

improve MPA effectiveness, increase local capacity, and foster sustainable development. Management effectiveness, and thus success of protection, were illustrated by the improved live coral cover percentages recorded for reefs under Coral Reef Rehabilitation and Management Programme (COREMAP) protection [122].

Regional Seas in East Asia

In 1977, on the initiative of the five states of the East Asian region (at the time), Indonesia, Malaysia, Philippines, Singapore, and Thailand, the Governing Council of UNEP decided that 'steps are urgently needed to formulate and establish a scientific programme involving research, prevention, and control of marine pollution and monitoring,' i.e. a regional action plan in East Asia (Decision 88(v)) [123].

The Coordinating Body on the Seas of East Asia (COBSEA), comprising Australia, Cambodia, China, Indonesia, Malaysia, Myanmar, Philippines, Singapore, Thailand, and Vietnam, is responsible for guiding, by a regular intergovernmental meeting, the Action Plan for the Protection and Development of the Marine Environment and Coastal Areas of the East Asian Seas Region. The Action Plan, which does not have a Convention, is administered by its Secretariat, the Regional Coordinating Unit (EAS/RCU), located in Bangkok, Thailand [109].

ICRAN in East Asia

ICRAN activities in the region target capacity development in reef management through transfer of lessons learned and experiences gained at selected sites (Bunaken Island (Indonesia), Mu Koh Surin (Thailand), Apo Island Marine Reserve (Philippines), Komodo Island (Indonesia)) to a number of target sites (Ninh Thuan (Vietnam), Sanya (China), Koh Rong (Cambodia), Gili Islands (Indonesia)). For reefs under successful management, three different regimes were chosen: (1) ICZM, (2) ecotourism, and (3) community-based management. In addition, UNEP's EAS/RCU manages a system of small grants to enhance coral-reef monitoring activities in the region. ICRAN, in partnership with UNEP EAS/RCU, also hosted a regional 'Workshop to Establish Networks of Marine Protected Areas in the East Asian Seas Region' whilst the World Commission on Protected Areas (WCPA), TNC, and the National Oceanic and Atmospheric Administration (NOAA) jointly devised a project aimed at strengthening and improving the effectiveness of MPAs through the development of a Regional Action Plan (RAP).

The ICRAN regional workshop held in Phuket, Thailand, in August 2002, provided a forum for site managers in East Asia to exchange experiences and lessons learned in management, as well as best practices. It also provided participants with the opportunity to present results of assessment of management schemes and existing legislation, and to discuss how successful practices at one site could be translated into action on the ground in other areas.

Solution Strategies of the Alternative Income Increase in Gili Matra Marine Natural Recreation Park (GM-MNRP) West Nusa Tenggara Province – Indonesia

Edi Djuharsa

Background

Gili Matra Marine Natural Recreation Park (GM-MNRP) is located off the north-western coast of Lombok, in the West Nusa Tenggara Province of Indonesia. Encompassing a total area of approximately 30 km2, the park consists of three islands: Gili Meno (1.5 km2), Gili Air (1.75 km2), and Gili Trawangan (3.4 km2), also encompassing 22.9 km2 of marine area. The park is host to vast expanses of seagrass beds and coral reefs characterized by high live-coral cover [124].

The area was designated as park in 1993, based on a proposal from the Governor of West Nusa Tenggara Province. Gili is managed through the Natural Resources Conservation Office of West Nusa Tenggara (Balai Konservasi Sumber Daya Alam Nusa Tenggara Barat) under the Directorate of Forest Protection and Nature Conservation, Ministry of Forestry Indonesia. The management objectives are based on the Conservation of Living Resources and their Ecosystems Act. There are a number of Indonesian laws that directly pertain to the establishment of Gili Matra as a marine park, including several national and traditional community rules concerning fisheries, management, protected areas, rehabilitation, mining, and the protection of marine resources in general [124].

The main management objectives for Gili are to promote sustainable use of the Park's resources through: 'local participation in park management to protect biological values of the park, the elimination of further disturbances or alteration of natural habitats, protection of endangered and threatened animal species inclusive of their habitats, maintenance of areas selected for recreation and tourism development, sustainable use of commercial fish habitats, and sustainable use and careful management of species and their habitats.' [124]

Issues and topics covered

Stakeholder Involvement, Empowerment and Community Support

Zoning and Conflict Resolution

Sustainable Management of Resources

Public Awareness and Education

Sustainable Financing

Enforcement and Compliance

Developing a Conservation Strategy for Gili Matra

The establishment of Gili Matra as a marine park stemmed from the recognition that marine and coastal resources, especially coral reefs, are potentially valuable assets that can be used towards marine tourism development, in turn improving the welfare and income of locals in the West Lombok district. However, unregulated population growth, lack of information, awareness, technical guidance, means, facilities, expertise, and human resources, have resulted in ongoing conflicts between new management objectives and development activities. One of the major threats to the area's reefs is the regular use by local fishers of destructive fishing techniques such as poison, blast fishing, and muro-ami. As a result, disputes have arisen between stakeholders, particularly between fishers and members of the tourism industry. These conflicts have also been partly fuelled by the lack of awareness, from related institutions and parties, of the park's boundaries and zones.

It has been recognised that the success of GM-MNRP depends on the ongoing development of a management plan, arrived at through an extensive and collaborative process involving all stakeholders: the community, NGOs, tourism business players, village authorities, and sub-districts, and with the help and advice of Bunaken National Park, its ICRAN paired site in Indonesia. Such a process will help clarify management objectives and provide a framework for conflict resolution and enforcement. There is also a need to increase public awareness of Gili Matra's park status as well as provide training and education to all stakeholders (only 10% have high-school education [124]).

A conservation strategy for Gili was developed by taking into account sources of conflict, the park's potential value, the establishment of regulations, as well as environmental and socio-economic conditions of surrounding communities. To date, the strategic plan encompasses: the promotion of management activities for the park and its resources; capacity building; providing assistance to local communities to find alternate sources of income; increasing awareness in the local community in relation to the potential

Table 5

CASE STUDIES

benefits of the park; and strengthening coordination among related institutions and parties. Each strategy is being detailed in a five-year action plan providing a basis for management activities. An annual plan is used to obtain funding from the government for technical cooperation with other institutions. Although specific activities in action plans may vary from year to year, the basic programme structure remains the same (Table 5).

Table 5 – Basic action plan structure

Programme	Activities
Conservation Planning	Annual plan preparation· Development of activities programme
Monitoring and inventory	Coral reef monitoring and inventory Database development and management
Biodiversity management and safeguarding	Hawksbill turtle semi-natural hatching programme Artificial reef establishment· Integration of operations Regular patrolling
Data and information	Evaluation of visitor numbers, disturbances, and park biodiversity
Manpower management	Development of training programmes
Facilities	Maintenance and provision of facilities and equipment
Community awareness	Coordination meetings on planning and sustainable utilization Conservation education and extension Conservation exhibitions· Information dissemination
Community development	Local management of marine areas

Strategic planning has resulted in a number of management successes in Gili:

- Development of a ten-year management plan 1998-2008.

- Establishment of protected and harvested areas.

- Formation of the Education of Youth Conservation Group that then forms the Youth Front Foundation of Taskforce Gili Patrols.

- Arrest and prosecution (nine months in jail) of fish-bombers as a result of a joint protection operation between West Nusa Tenggara Natural Resources Conservation Office, the Police, and the Community (Taskforce Gili Patrols).

- Implementation of an agreement between coastal communities in Northwest Lombok. The document was signed by local community leaders, the heads of Tanjung District, Gangga District, and Pemenang District. It establishes the Foundation of the Fisherman Community Organization in Northern West Lombok with the goal to assist in implementing coastal security activities by Taskforce Gili Patrols, and to develop and implement traditional ruling (awiq awiq), defining procedures of enforcement and penalties for offences (maximum penalty Rp. 10,000,000, ca. US$1,160).

- Deployment of park boundary buoys, conducting of daily patrols, construction of infrastructure for coastal security activities, and provision of help on community awareness and sustainable use of marine resources campaigns, all implemented by community members (with NGO support).

- Implementation of a sea-turtle conservation programme.

Partnerships and stakeholder involvement have allowed GM-MNRP to build on its successes and to strengthen existing programmes through collaboration and cooperation with national institutions. For example, West Nusa Tenggara Natural Resources Conservation Office, in cooperation with Mataram University and a number of NGOs, conducted a coral-reef census, whilst a collaborative operation between Diponegoro University, Mataram University, and West Nusa Tenggara Natural Resources Conservation Office developed audiovisual documentation. Community members have also joined forces to establish environmental conservation groups with the aim to reduce the amount of organic and inorganic pollutants entering the marine environment. Finally, cooperation between Taskforce Gili Patrols and West Nusa Tenggara Natural Resources Conservation Office has led to the development of buffer-zone areas where coral transplantation experiments are being carried out.

Future Efforts

Although there has been some success in establishing Gili Matra as a marine park, it has been difficult to quantify benefits resulting from park management due to limited resources, infrastructure, and ongoing conflicts between stakeholders. Future efforts to increase the quality of marine resources in the context of community welfare through tourism are needed. Ongoing efforts are focusing on continuing to build local involvement through training and education. There is also a need to develop a support infrastructure for enforcement officers. Public awareness of zoning regulations needs to be increased, and coordination among stakeholders requires further development. Moreover, increased technical and non-technical assistance is required from domestic and international NGOs. The implementation of such continuing efforts will require the participation of all stakeholders and governing bodies, as well as additional support from the Indonesian government to strengthen relationships with international NGOs.

LESSONS LEARNED

Stakeholder Involvement, Empowerment and Community Support

- All stakeholders, though a participatory and cooperative process, should reach a compromise and develop sets of management objectives they agree upon.

- Representation of small as well as large groups is warranted.

- Roles and responsibilities should be clearly defined, as otherwise conservation management will suffer from competition over authority or differences in goals.

Partnerships in Management

- Involvement of the private sector in MPA management should be secured, as it can be highly beneficial both from the perspective of financial support as well as human capacity.

- Support from local government institutions should be sought, as it can help in strengthening ties to international NGOs.

- Collaboration and cooperation with national institutions should be strengthened.

Zoning and Conflict Resolution

- Zoning regulations should be simple, clearly defined, and effectively communicated to all stakeholders.

- Zoning boundaries should be well demarcated and enforced.

Public Awareness and Education

- Awareness raising campaigns should be established.

- Training and education of local stakeholders should be provided.

Sustainable Financing

- Sufficient resources should be made available, and adequate infrastructure put in place.

- Collaborative efforts at a community as well as national level should be established to gain financial support at a national, regional and international level.

Enforcement and Compliance

- A firm enforcement system (preferably which encompasses traditional ruling should be set up.

Development of Management Plans

- A management plan should be developed, as an important step towards securing funding from governmental as well as other institutions.

- A management plan should be arrived at though an extensive and collaborative process involving all stakeholders.

- A management plan should include information pertaining to ecological as well as socio-economic data of surrounding communities.

The Bunaken National Park Co-Management Initiative

Maxi Wowiling and Roy Pangalila

Background

Bunaken National Park (BNP) is a MPA on the coast of North Sulawesi, Indonesia, located north and south of the major city of Manado. The park covers a total area of 890 km², of which 97% is marine, divided between the northern and southern parts of the park. The terrestrial portion includes patches of mainland and five islands in the north (Bunaken, Manado Tua, Mantehage, Nain and Siladen). BNP is renowned for its high levels of biodiversity and underwater geological structure. The area contains a wide array of habitat types such as coral reefs, mangroves, seagrass, deep coastal waters, seawalls, and trenches which support a diversity of species including corals (70 genera), reef-fish communities, dugongs, sea turtles, and a newly discovered group of resident coelacanths. It has been estimated that about 70% of the fish species occurring in the Indo-Western Pacific can be found in the park [125].

> **Issues and topics covered**
>
> Stakeholder Involvement, Empowerment and Community Support
>
> Partnerships for Management
>
> Alternative Livelihoods and Socio-economic Issues
>
> Zoning and Conflict Resolution
>
> Enforcement and Compliance
>
> Capacity Building
>
> Sustainable Financing
>
> Monitoring

Over 30,000 residents live in 22 villages within the park boundaries, and many more in surrounding areas. These communities depend largely on natural resources from the park or nearby areas for food and as a source of income [126]. The park has also become one of the most well-known ecotourism destinations, serving primarily the dive industry: 20 dive operators see an estimated 20,000 visitors per year, generating approximately US$4.4 million [127]. BNP also contributes roughly US$3.8 million/year in fisheries and seaweed aquaculture production to the North Sulawesi economy [127].

In 1991, Bunaken was declared a national park by the central Indonesian government [125]. Although the area had been declared a local and provincial protected area prior to 1991, no organized management authority was put in place to coordinate activities and enforce regulations in the park. A 25-year management plan, promoting the conservation of the park's biodiversity, the development of sustainable ecotourism benefiting the local economy, and the improvement of locals' lifestyle through the sustainable management of their resources, was developed and published in 1996 by the national government [126]. It was to provide a managing authority, including park rangers, and limited funds to regulate the park and ensure enforcement of legislative measures [126]. Management authority for the park is vested in the BNP Office, which is controlled by the national-level Department of Nature Conservation [127].

Since its inception in 1991, BNP has been faced with a number of management challenges. Destructive fishing and farming practices as well as rapid and poorly planned coastal development have resulted in ecological damage to the aquatic and terrestrial habitats. Unethical business and political practices resulted in unequal distribution of revenues generated from natural resources in the park. Mistrust amongst local stakeholders and managers, as well as unorganized management strategies, have resulted in poor compliance with management objectives and unclear zoning regulations. Increasing demands from stakeholders for fair and accountable management led to the development of a representative management advisory board (effectively a co-management strategy) to manage revenues generated from the newly established entrance-fee system, and to coordinate patrols, as well as conservation and development activities, in the park [126]. The fee system, aimed at allowing the BNP Authority to be fully self-financed in the long-term, came into force in 2001. 80% of the revenue generated from it goes to

activities supporting specific conservation programmes in the park, including enforcement, conservation education, waste management, and environmentally friendly village development, whilst the remaining 20% are split between local, provincial, and national government [128]. Central to the management plan is also a multiple-use zonation system, legally mandated in Indonesia's 1990 Biodiversity Conservation Act, which requires that management of Indonesia's national park system be based upon zonation plans [127]. Since the implementation of the park, the United States Agency for International Development (USAID) Natural Resources Management (NRM) Project has provided technical assistance for the development of the park management plan (including the zonation system) and support to the eventual zonation revision process [127].

Co-management Initiative

Since 1998, USAID's NRM Programme has been working actively to implement a co-management initiative in the park and instil a sense of ownership of local resources in the park's main stakeholders. The goal of this initiative is to develop an effective and sustainably-financed Indonesian model of multi-stakeholder co-management of a national marine park. The key to achieving this goal has been a massive socialization effort to draw the various stakeholders from the park (including villagers, an active marine tourism industry, local conservation NGOs, academia, and three tiers of government agencies) into a single 'community' with a strong sense of awareness and ownership of the valuable, but threatened, marine resources in the park. A multimedia park socialization campaign has been implemented to encourage a sense of ownership in local communities, through the use of posters, zoning calendars, town hall meetings, community information billboards, a 30 base station VHF community radio network, local television shows, and local, national, and international newspapers, and magazine articles. A number of other initiatives have also been undertaken. For example, NRM/EPIQ (Environmental Policy and Institutional Strengthening (EPIQ)) is assisting the BNP Authority (Bunaken National Park Office) to work with the other two primary park user groups (local villagers and the marine tourism sector) to revise the park's zoning system. NRM/EPIQ is also providing technical assistance to the North Sulawesi Watersports Association and actively fostering the involvement of other private sector groups (cottage owners, traditional fishers' association, and charter boat operators) in BNP management.

Moreover, NRM/EPIQ has been providing development support to the BNP Management Advisory Board (DPTNB), which consists of representatives from national, provincial, and local government agencies, village stakeholders, the private tourism sector, academia, and environmental NGOs, and has been facilitating multi-stakeholder co-management of BNP. Villager involvement was improved upon in BNP management decisions through the institutional development of the BNP Concerned Citizen's Forum, active in all 22 villages in BNP. Its development has served to represent the aspirations of about 30,000 villagers in management decisions, as well as serving to socialize management policy to its constituents. An experimental joint 24-hour patrol system, involving park rangers, water-police officers, and local villagers has proven highly effective in decreasing destructive fishing practices in the park. Finally, in conjunction with WWF Wallacea, NRM/EPIQ is providing support to park stakeholders in monitoring coral condition (using manta tows and line intercept transects) and reef fish stocks (visual census and monitoring of Grouper and Napoleon Wrasse spawning aggregation sites), in an effort to institutionalize a scientific monitoring programme to observe effects of management activities on park resources.

Although the co-management process in BNP is a work in progress, there have been a number of successful endeavours to date. Participatory zoning revisions have been completed for Bunaken and Manado Tua Islands and are ongoing in 18 villages. While BNP's original zonation system utilized eight different zone types, stakeholder groups argued strongly to reduce this to three types that reflect the three primary values of the park (i.e. conservation, tourism, and fisheries values) [127]. Thus, the new zoning regulation simplified a complex 'jigsaw' structure of multiple zones to three primary zones with a clear definition of regulations in each zone, reflecting a compromise between user groups. The strict conservation and tourism use zones are both 'no-take' and were sited to include known reef fish spawning aggregation sites, unique reef features, and long-established dive sites [127]. Fishers agreed to these 20% closures after care was taken to thoroughly explain the fisheries-enhancing benefits of no-take zones [127]. As a result, compliance with zoning regulation has been high and an 11.1% increase in coral cover has been recorded in 18 months. Increases in size and abundance of commercially valuable fish species have also been reported [126, 127]. Institutionalization of the 15-seat multi-stakeholder Management Advisory Board and the 22-village BNP Concerned Citizen's Forum has improved communication between all interest groups. Strong participation of the private sector in park management through the North Sulawesi Watersports Association has resulted in a commitment to increasing employment of locals, participation in educational programmes, and assistance with park enforcement. This programme has been dubbed the 'three E's' – employment, education, and enforcement. Development of a decentralized park entrance-fee system succeeded in raising US$42,000 in its first year of operation (2001), US$109,000 in its second year, and is targeting up to US$250,000 a year in the future. Implementation of a joint patrol system involving villagers and park rangers has virtually eradicated blast and cyanide fishing from the park, and greatly limited illegal coral mining and mangrove cutting.

In 2003, BNP was voted global winner of British Airways Tourism for Tomorrow awards, beating more than 70 other entrants in the worldwide competition [129]. Lessons learned from the co-management process for BNP have been shared with MPA managers from Bali Barat National Park, Komodo National Park, Wakatobi National Park, Cenderawasih National Park, Berau Islands, Tomini Bay, and Gili Matra Marine Natural Recreation Park, its ICRAN paired site in Indonesia, and Hon Mun Marine Reserve in Vietnam.

However, it should be highlighted that the past two years of terrorist attacks, political instability, and worldwide health scares have led to a global tourism downturn that is also impacting protected areas around the globe that depend on user fees as a source of conservation funding. BNP, for example, collected less than half of its targeted 2003 revenues. Interestingly, the downturn in revenue generated by international visitors (in Bunaken, arrivals are down 13% from last year) masks the highly significant surge in domestic tourism experienced by national parks in the region. This experience has highlighted the danger of relying too heavily upon entrance fees for sustainable long-term financing of a park's operational costs [130].

LESSONS LEARNED

Stakeholder Involvement, Empowerment and Community Support

- Establishment of a sense of pride and ownership of local marine resources (or the management of those resources) engenders strong conservation support.

- All relevant stakeholders should be involved in co-management, and this needs to be site-specific.

- Long-term stakeholders provide better solutions and support for conservation management.

- The composition of multi-stakeholder co-management boards is critical to success, giving less vocal/vociferous groups greater representation.

- Representation of larger groups (villages, private sector) needs to be continuously facilitated as they often neglect their responsibilities or are resented by their constituencies.

- More focused, smaller group meetings should be held, as well as larger village meetings, to involve more marginalized or traditionally quiet community members.

- Campaigns in schools, mosques and churches are effective for gaining local support.

- Monitoring and evaluation are essential for convincing stakeholders that conservation works, or for directing changes when it is less effective.

- Both the ecological and socio-economic values of coral reefs should be emphasised to gain political stakeholder support.

- Development-oriented/government stakeholders need to see conservation in a regional economic context.

Partnerships for Management

- The involvement of many diverse stakeholder groups in management can prevent corruption and ensure that management supports stakeholders' objectives.

- Involvement of the private sector can be highly beneficial, as members can be the strongest proponents of good management and provide considerable financial and human resources.

- Co-management only happens when partnerships are truly constituency-based and then begin to work together.

continued...

...continued

- Decentralization of conservation management only works when roles and responsibilities are clear, not when there is competition over management authority, or when differences in goals exist.

Capacity Building

- Training in community facilitation skills for park management personnel is essential for stakeholder support and for ensuring that communities understand park objectives.

- Long-term 'learning-by-doing' training is more effective than specific technical training programmes.

Zoning and Conflict Resolution

- When developing a zoning plan, active involvement of user groups and a spirit of compromise are crucial to success.

- Clear zonation plans are useful for mitigating conflict between stakeholders and balancing conservation with sustainable development (especially where population pressures are large).

- Zonation schemes should have a minimal number of clearly explained and marked zones, and explicit rules for each zone.

Alternative Livelihoods and Socio-economic Issues

- Alternative livelihood programmes aimed at stakeholders involved in destructive activities are ineffective and tend to be largely rejected by local communities.

Enforcement and Compliance

- Community stakeholders should support patrol and enforcement programmes because they are directly linked to increased livelihoods.

- Community programmes should focus on rewarding those that have chosen sustainable livelihoods, and deal with destructive members of the community by means of a strong enforcement system.

- Joint patrol systems, involving villagers and park rangers, can help decrease destructive fishing practices in a park.

Sustainable Financing

- Self-financing systems are essential for providing local stakeholders with the capacity to manage local conservation initiatives, and generate and manage finances locally.

- Tourists are generally willing to pay reasonably high entrance fees as long as they can see the results in visible conservation management, i.e. fees should be earmarked for conservation and monitoring programmes and/or related activities.

- Reliance on a single source of funding for conservation management (e.g. tourism) is risky – funding mechanisms should be diverse.

Monitoring

- Collaboration efforts in monitoring can help institutionalize a programme aimed at observing effects of management objectives on park resources.

PART VIII. THE SOUTH PACIFIC REGION

The tropical southwest and southeast Pacific covers a vast area of the planet, with states and/or territories scattered over a large number of islands. The region accounts for 13% of the world's coral reefs – fringing, barrier, platform, and atolls – and hosts incredible biodiversity.

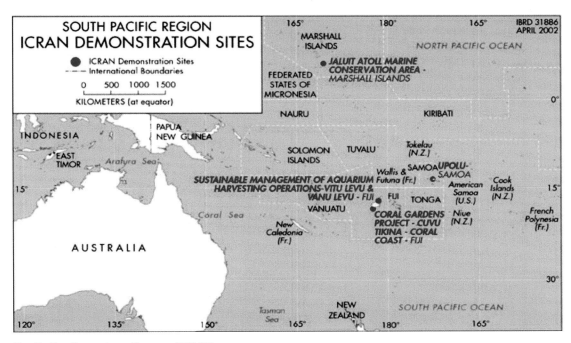

South Pacific region. Source: ICRAN

The Region – Habitat, Population, and Economic Characteristics

Many Pacific Islanders whose languages, knowledge, traditional beliefs, and practices emphasise a close connection between people and their environment, particularly the sea, live close to the ocean in dispersed village communities. In countries such as the Solomon Islands, Papua New Guinea, and Fiji, an estimated three quarters of people living in rural communities have little or no cash income, depending almost entirely on natural and particularly marine resources for survival. A subsistence economy still dominates most Pacific Islands, with data from some islands having shown that an estimated 90% of families go fishing at least once a week, and many nearly every day [131]. For thousands of years, Pacific islanders have lived a relatively sustainable way of life, with species and habitat recovery not representing new concepts to them [132].

Fish catch on Dravuni, Fiji.
© Rebecca Mitchell

Many cultures traditionally applied restrictions on the use of key resources as they became scarce, reopening exploitation of them once they had replenished. Part of a system known as customary marine tenure, these structures are still prevalent in most countries of the South Pacific. They are chiefly based on ancestral rights and are administered at different levels within communities [133]. However, in countries where these have broken down, modern influences have led to the development of governance systems that tend to stress resources as common property, and, in many instances, have brought about unsustainable exploitation of marine resources [133]. Moreover, populations, currently totalling 6 million people and expected to double within the next 20 years [132], are expanding rapidly and applying increasing levels of pressure on marine

Giant clam. © Cedric Genevois

and coastal systems. To target these issues, social researchers and scientists have promoted the implementation of MPAs and the development of marine resource and integrated coastal zone management plans, which recognise certain traditional marine regulations [133] and incorporate them into contemporary management. A number of marine conservation areas have been designated throughout the region with varying levels of success. Experience has shown that MPAs implemented after having followed a careful collaborative process, fully engaging resource owners, and whose plans are based on co-management of resources, have tended to be the most effective.

Reef-monitoring programmes in the region (with the exception perhaps of Fiji, due to the presence of the main campus of the University of the South Pacific (USP) and a number of NGOs; New Caledonia; and French Polynesia) have been hindered by poor coordination and knowledge of marine resources, lack of financial resources and capacity [132], and lack of political will. However, efforts within the last three years have been made to secure financial assistance (e.g. Conservation Action Fund, Canada South Pacific Ocean Development Programme, and the International Ocean Institute) towards standardized and regular monitoring of reef habitats and assessments of their stocks. Reefs of Micronesia and American Samoa are included in a number of programmes under the auspices of the US Coral Reef Task Force, and as such have also benefited from improved mapping, monitoring, and training activities.

The condition of South Pacific reefs is highly variable, with reefs in Fiji, Polynesia, and the Cook Islands, situated particularly close to urban centres, suffering from the effects of pollution, sedimentation, dredging, heavy gleaning, mining, refuse disposal, and coastal development. On the other hand, in Niue, Palau, and many atoll countries, there has been little reef disturbance from activities other than harvesting. Increasing consumption of marine organisms and their derived products has meant that fishing pressure in the South Pacific has been on the increase to meet the demand. Pressures from Asian markets have also been associated with increases in the use of destructive fishing practices (e.g. poison, dynamite, and night spear fishing) in the region (e.g. Solomon Islands [133], Fiji, Marshall Islands, and Kiribati [134]), even on the most remote reefs [135]. With increased concern amongst hobbyists over unsustainable aquarium organism collection practices in Indonesia, pressure from the rapidly expanding aquarium trade has moved export of live reef products to countries in the South Pacific, e.g. Kiribati, Cook Islands Solomon Islands, Vanuatu, and Tonga, and particularly Fiji. With the aim to better regulate the trade in marine aquarium organisms, management plans, monitoring protocols, and harvest policies are being discussed between a number of government authorities, wholesalers, NGOs, and regulatory boards (e.g. the Marine Aquarium Council (MAC)).

Tourism development in the region has also been seen as a potentially sustainable income earner. However, development activities on some islands have resulted in major degradation, recognised cultural impacts, and, at times, led to conflicts between operators and communities over access to lagoon and reef resources [136].

Threats to the South Pacific reefs' integrity through over-exploitation (particularly of giant clams, sea cucumbers, and trochus shells [135]) have been aggravated by recent catastrophes such as coral bleaching and crown of thorns outbreaks [131]. Although reefs were not particularly affected by the 1997-98 El Niño event, significant coral bleaching and mortality in the first three months of 2002 were observed in New Caledonia, Vanuatu, Fiji, Samoa, the Cook Islands, and French Polynesia [137]. This is following already high mortality levels due to bleaching in 2000. However, many affected reefs are making a strong recovery [133].

South Pacific Regional Environment Programme (SPREP)

In the South Pacific, ICRAN's activities and actions are facilitated chiefly through SPREP. The programme was set up as an inter-governmental regional organization in 1986 by the governments and administrations of the Pacific, through the UNEP Regional Seas Programme, to coordinate and facilitate the sustainable use of the region's natural resources [138]. SPREP's headquarters are located in Apia, Western Samoa, and are headed by a Director who reports to the Intergovernmental Meeting of SPREP member states, comprising Australia, Cook Islands, Federated States of Micronesia, Fiji, France, Kiribati, Marshall Islands, Nauru, New Zealand, Niue, Palau, Papua New Guinea, Solomon Islands, Tonga, Tuvalu, United Kingdom, United States of America, Vanuatu, and Western Samoa [109]. The organization has grown from a small programme attached to the South Pacific Commission in the 1980s into one of the region's major inter-governmental organizations [139].

SPREP's activities are guided by the Action Plan for Managing the Environment of the South Pacific as well as the Convention for the Protection of the Natural Resources and Environment of the South Pacific Region [138]. The development and implementation of the Action Plan is the responsibility of the 26 countries and territories that make up the region (all 22 Pacific island countries and territories, and four developed countries with direct interests in the region: Australia, France, New Zealand, and the United States of America) [138]. SPREP has been assisting countries to comply with Conventions and Agreements on marine conservation and sustainable development, by targeting mainly five areas: education and awareness; monitoring, assessment and research; capacity building; legislation; and the creation of networks and sharing of experiences between communities and amongst programmes [133]. Some of SPREP's current projects include [140]:

- *The International Waters Programme*: the Pacific Islands Climate Change Assistance Programme (PICCAP) and the Climate Change Training Programme (CC:TRAIN) projects are aimed at assisting Pacific Island countries to meet their obligations under Articles 4 and 12 of the UN Framework Convention on Climate Change (UNFCCC). These projects are funded by the GEF through UNDP; CC:TRAIN is executed by the UN Institute for Training and Research (UNITAR) in close collaboration with the Climate Change Secretariat and UNEP's Information Unit on Conventions (UNEP IUC).

- *Waste Management Education and Awareness* with support provided by the European Union.

- *Climate Change and Environmental Education and Training* programmes with assistance from the Australian Agency for International Development (AusAID).

- *Atmospheric and Radiation Measurements in the Tropical Western Pacific* sponsored by the US Department of Energy.

- *Capacity Building for Sustainable Development in the South Pacific*: Building on the National Environment Management Strategies (NEMS) Capacity 21, a UNDP programme launched at the 1992 UNCED, which works with developing countries and countries in transition to find the best ways to achieve sustainable development and meet the goals of Agenda 21. The latter is a statement of willingness, signed in 1992 by 178 countries, to strive for a form of development that recognises the essential links between economic growth, social equity and environmental protection [141].

- *The environmental clearing-house* functions of SPREP operating with funding provided by the government of New Zealand.

- *Studies* to assess the feasibility (ecological and socio-economic) of the coral trade in Fiji and Solomon Islands.

Over the past four years, in recognition of the value of MPAs as an important tool in marine conservation and management of coastal and marine resources, a range of national and community based coastal reserves have been declared, or established, by local communities, with the help of regional and national organizations [138]. However, most MPAs in the region are ineffective, and thus failing to achieve the conservation objectives for which they were established. The main reasons for this include insufficient funding, lack of capacity, insufficient data, and lack of information exchange. It is to note that a few MPAs and coastal sites within the region are currently implementing management practices and approaches successfully, which could be adapted, where appropriate, by other sites with similar issues [138]. ICRAN supports a range of sites and activities in the region: Samoa MPA Project (Savai'I and Upolu Islands), Jaluit Atoll Marine Conservation Area (Marshall Islands), Sustainable Management of Aquarium Harvesting Operations (Fiji), the Coral Gardens Project (Fiji and Solomon Islands), Rock Islands Southern Lagoon Management Project, Tokelau Marine Resource Management Project, American Samoa Village Fisheries Management Project, National Locally Managed Marine Area Networks (Fiji and Solomon Islands), and the Regional Locally Managed Marine Area Network.

CASE STUDIES

Multiple-use Management Plan for Whole of Atoll Management: Jaluit Atoll Marine Conservation Area Management Plan

John Bungitak, Mary Power and Miriam Philip

'We, the Jaluit community, our traditional leaders and elected representatives, are concerned over ever increasing trends of resource depletion within our atoll. We want to develop a Management Plan that will protect our environment while allowing sustainable use of our atoll's natural resources'

– Call from Jaluit Atoll community in the Marshall Islands in 2002.

Background

The atolls of the Marshall Islands run north and south in two parallel chains. The eastern chain is called Ratak (sunrise), whilst the western chain bears the name of Ralik (sunset). At the southern end of the Ralik island chain lies Jaluit Atoll, composed of 91 small islands (with a total land area of only 11.4 km²) forming a ring around a shallow lagoon (690 km²) that connects to the ocean via four deep passes. Marine biodiversity is high, with over 250 species of fish, and numerous species of invertebrates having been found to inhabit the atoll, along with four species of mangroves, several species of turtles, whales, and dolphins [142].

The 2,500 inhabitants of Jaluit Atoll mainly reside on six of the 91 islands. The island's economy is based primarily on subsistence activities, with all communities relying heavily on natural resources (copra, giant clams, trochus, sea cucumbers, finfish, blacklip pearl oysters, and turtles) as a source of food and income [142]. Recent surveys found exploitation levels of giant clams, trochus, sea cucumbers, and oysters to be unsustainable.

> **Issues and topics covered**
>
> Stakeholder Participation, Empowerment and Community Support
>
> Sustainable Management of Resources
>
> Tourism and Sustainable Development
>
> Zoning and Conflict Resolution
>
> Development of Management Plans
>
> Monitoring
>
> Partnerships for Management
>
> Alternative Livelihoods and Socio-economic Issues
>
> Public awareness and Education
>
> Capacity Building

These results were confirmed by questionnaires filled out by the community, which highlighted (80% of respondents) that these animals were becoming scarce and that they would welcome and support a conservation programme [143]. Population stock abundances of finfish are high, and current subsistence harvesting levels do not appear to be detrimental to these populations. Traditional methods are still prevalent on the islands and apply in particular to specific zones established under local custom which prescribe that only island chiefs, on special occasions, are allowed access to resources in those areas [144].

Marine Conservation Area

Following preliminary studies carried out in 1998, the Jaluit Atoll Conservation Area (JACA) was established, in 1999, under the Republic of the Marshall Islands Environmental Protection Authority (RMIEPA), in partnership with GEF and SPREP (through its South Pacific Biodiversity Conservation Programme (SPBCP)). JACA's main objectives are to assist in marine and coastal conservation, whilst ensuring sustainable use, by local communities, of natural resources. Combined efforts by the Jaluit Atoll Development Association, the Jaluit Atoll Local Government Council, and the Jaluit Community assisted in the development of JACA [143]. A Conservation Area Supporting Officer (CASO), based on Jaluit Atoll, has recently been appointed to manage and

Jaluit Atoll Conservation Area (JACA). © SPREP

develop the programme [143]. He is assisted by a Conservation Area Coordinating Committee, along with the General Manager of the Environmental Protection Authority in the Marshall Islands that has the Atoll mayor as chairman, and senior traditional leaders in the island council as members.

Aims of the Conservation Area are to develop and implement:

- A sustainable marine resource management plan.

- A sustainable terrestrial management plan.

- A community-based management system.

- Alternative livelihood activities.

- Public awareness, training and education programmes, and measures to strengthen the capacity of the community to effectively manage a conservation area.

Surveys conducted in 2000 showed that trochus, and sea cucumber stocks in particular, were suffering severe declines due to unsustainable harvest practices. It became apparent that in order to better protect these resources (whilst providing residents with a livelihood), a resource management plan was needed. In order to establish a practical and meaningful plan as well as a sound monitoring programme, a baseline census of species and habitat distribution was developed. Surveys carried out in 2001 assessed and estimated (using manta tows, timed swims, and line transects) live coral cover as well as stock levels for selected species of giant clams, trochus, blacklip pearl oysters, and finfish (e.g. groupers and rainbow runner). In addition, the general distribution of populations of giant clams, trochus, and blacklip pearl oysters, as well as any other pertinent biophysical information, were mapped. Results showed that population stock abundances of finfish were being exploited at sustainable subsistence levels, but that management protocols should be introduced for all species targeted for commercial purposes. Although stock abundances for giant clams were found to differ for each species, population numbers were in decline for all species (with suggestions of *T. gigas* and *T. derasa* being extinct from the atoll). Blacklip pearl oysters, located principally within the lagoon, are being collected for their shell, which is then used

in the button and handicraft trade. Keen interest to develop an industry for black pearl production has been expressed by members of the community, requiring the development of harvest, use, and trade regulations. Stock populations of trochus were low due to high recent levels of commercial harvesting. A total ban on exploitation of this species has been recommended until its recovery, at which time a sustainable harvesting system should be implemented. Sea cucumbers were found in high numbers, with the exception of five species as a result of commercial exploitation, calling for management protocols to be developed [143].

Mooring buoys used to delineate the no take zones.
© Gordon Lapraik

Following this baseline census, Jaluit, with initial support from SPREP-SPBCP, engaged experts who, over the course of two years, consulted with community members and formulated a small scale ecotourism strategy prior to developing the resource management plan itself [144]. One issue of particular importance to local residents, and mentioned repeatedly during meetings, was that of incorporating both traditional (such as 'MO', traditional closures) and modern conservation methods into the plan [144]. The whole of the atoll, rather than small sections, was designated as a conservation area, recognising that sustainable resource management, especially in a small-island context, will not work in isolation from the rest of the island ecosystem. Unfortunately, SPREP-SPBCP support started to phase out prior to the completion of an atoll-wide resource management plan. Funding provided by ICRAN allowed for the consultative process with local communities (during which they were given the chance to raise questions and concerns as well as exchange ideas) to be upheld. The resource management plan, which benefits from strong support by all community members, was finalized in early 2003. As part of the plan, a zoning management system, endorsed by RMIEPA, was devised. It combines traditional community-owned management areas with other scientific based zones, such as Sanctuary (No-take zones) and General Zones (extractive activities). Additional funding from the Netherlands Government helped staff raise awareness of the resource plan, train leaders in establishing management measures that relate to the plan, conduct public meetings to gain support for the measures set out in the plan, and establish training programmes for schools and local people in management activities as well as ongoing monitoring [144].

Accomplishments to Date

The main achievements to date include the completion and successful operation of the ecotourism component of the project and the construction of a walking trail around the mangrove forest. Eight traditional accommodation units, managed by local landowners, have begun operation. Staff have produced a brochure to promote the island and its activities, which include nature walks through mangrove forest, snorkelling and diving trips, canoe sailing, and a cultural tour [144]. The

Ecotourism guesthouse. © Mary Power

Jaluit Women's Handicraft Club has completed the handicraft shop on Jabor, established outlets in Majuro, and continues to conduct community beautification and cleanup activities in Jabor.

A grant from National Fish and Wildlife Foundation (NFWF) to 'Designate fisheries management areas for the Jaluit Atoll as part of a coordinated government marine resources management plan for the atoll' [145] and funds from RAMSAR towards 'Capacity building for implementation of the resource management plan for Jaluit Atoll Marine Protected Area' [146] were secured in 2002 and 2003, respectively. Mooring buoys have now been installed with the help of an expert to mark out the MO's and sanctuaries in the marine conservation area. In addition, RMIEPA's Education and Information Unit spent a week on the atoll in early 2003 to promote public awareness on conservation projects and solid waste management issues. The members of the unit also visited all the schools (including high schools and elementary schools) on the atoll, and as part of their awareness activities invited students to participate in art competitions. A marine resources monitoring team from the College of Marshall Islands also gave presentations to high school students and teachers of Jaluit, trained project officers and selected senior high-school students in coral reef monitoring and methods of data collection. An important result of such awareness-raising and educational activities is that fishermen are more aware of destructive fishing methods and gain a basic understanding of the biological aspects of the resources they harvest, thus helping and facilitating the promotion of sustainable fishing and resource-use methods [147].

Due to the successes registered on the island, increased interest by neighbouring communities have been expressed for the government to duplicate and extend conservation programmes such as that of Jaluit Atoll to their islands. When asked about the impact of ICRAN in Jaluit Atoll, John Bungitak, the General Manager of RMIEPA, said: 'To sum it up, not only has it helped to make the atoll's marine resources be sustainable for generations, but also other venues of income generation have been created, thus improving the quality of the peoples' lives on the atoll. ICRAN also has reactivated the dying tradition of conservation of the resources that the people had once practised since time immemorial.' [148]

Jaluit Women's Handicraft Club. © Mary Power

LESSONS LEARNED

Sustainable Management of Resources

- Incorporation of traditional conservation elements into a modern management framework is important in acquiring strong support of a resource management plan by community members.

- Designation of a whole atoll as a conservation area recognises that sustainable resource management will not work in isolation from the rest of the island's ecosystems.

- Successful MPA implementation will result in publicity; generate pride amongst community members, and stimulate interest in neighbouring islands to develop a similar system to tackle the issues they are facing.

- Development of harvest, use, and trade regulations can assist community members in exploiting resources sustainably.

- Species that demonstrate low population levels should be banned from exploitation.

- Clear management and regular monitoring protocols should be developed for species in decline.

Zoning and Conflict Resolution

- Zoning schemes, aimed at minimising resource-use conflicts, are most likely to be successfully supported by local community members if they incorporate traditional conservation elements.

- Mooring buoys should be used to clearly demarcate individual zones of a reserve.

Development of Management Plans

- Active participation by, and empowerment of, local communities in the development of a management plan to conserve and sustainably use their resources is key to the successful implementation of protected areas.

Monitoring

- Baseline and regular monitoring activities are important to establish the available resource base, examine fishing impacts on available stocks, develop sustainable exploitation levels, and examine impact of protection.

- Clear management and regular monitoring protocols should be developed for species in decline.

Alternative Livelihoods and Socio-economic Issues; Tourism and Sustainable Development

- The generation of alternative sources of income (e.g. ecotourism) can improve the lives of community members, as well as reduce dependence on marine resources as a revenue generator.

Public Awareness and Education

- Awareness raising and education campaigns help to promote sustainable fishing and resource use methods, by allowing fishermen to gain a basic understanding of the biological aspects of the resources they harvest and the true impacts of destructive fishing methods.

Coral Transplantation and Restocking to Accelerate the Recovery of Coral Reef Habitats and Fisheries Resources within No-Take Marine Protected Areas: Hands-on Approaches to Support Community-Based Coral Reef Management

Austin Bowden-Kerby

Background

Rural fishing communities are often implicated in routine practices that break and kill corals, leading to serious coral reef decline [149]. Among these problems are blast fishing [150, 151]; fishing net damage [152]; anchor damage [153]; dredging and sand mining [152, 154, 155]; and coral harvesting for lime production [156-158], for use as building materials [156, 158], and for commercial sale as curios or for the aquarium trade [159-161]. All of these destructive practices convert rocky reef substrata into unconsolidated rubble beds, with very little hope for natural recovery [162-166].

Even where reefs are left relatively intact, over-fishing alone can cause basic shifts in ecological functioning, resulting in decreased coral cover and lower biodiversity [167-171]. Management plans addressing over-fishing must be implemented as part of coral reef rehabilitation, restoring the ecological balance required to reverse coral reef decline.

In recent years, widespread coral-reef decline has inspired various governmental and NGO initiatives to conserve reefs, and traditional 'tabu' areas have begun to be re-established in several areas by chiefs and communities, often facilitated by these agencies.

Issues and topics covered
Stakeholder Involvement and Community Support
Sustainable Management of Resources
Partnerships for Management
Capacity Building; Public Awareness and Education
Monitoring

Natural Processes of Coral Reef Recovery

Attempting to restore degraded coral reefs requires a basic understanding of the natural recovery process, as well as knowledge of the conditions under which these natural processes succeed or fail. Coral reefs can take as long as 20-50 years to recover from severe damage [158, 172-174]. However, reefs often recover in 5-10 years, or less, when numerous corals and coral fragments survive [175-177]. The availability of suitable substrata for larval recruitment can limit coral reef recovery and restrict reef development, as coral larvae require specific types of rocky settlement substrata [178-180]. Recruitment of coral larvae is inhibited where substrata have become unstable [156, 163, 164], are overgrown by algae [181-183], or covered with a fine layer of sand or silt [184-186]. Even where the substratum is ideal for larval settlement, poor larval supply may sometimes limit coral reef recovery [150, 163, 187].

Coral Transplantation to Accelerate Natural Recovery Processes

Transplanting coral fragments has been suggested as a means to rehabilitate reefs by bypassing the critical early stages of coral recruitment, especially on substrata not favourable to larval recruitment or to post-recruitment survival [163, 166]. Coral fragments have a distinct advantage over newly-settled larval recruits due to their considerably larger size, having increased survival and growth rates [188], increased ability to compete for space [189, 190], and greater stability on unconsolidated substrata [163, 176, 191].

Various transplantation methods have been attempted with the goal of restoring coral cover to reefs. Much of the restoration efforts to date have focused on responding to acute episodes of damage, in particular the repair of reefs subsequent to ship groundings. Most of these efforts are located in high-energy reef-front areas, using expensive methods and requiring hundreds of hours underwater to secure dislodged coral colonies. Relatively little consideration has been given to the fact that the high-energy environments most often affected are normally dominated by stable sediment-free substrata where natural recruitment and recovery processes are most active, potentially making restoration efforts in these habitats unnecessary [192-197] (but see section further below). Recent re-evaluations of the successes and failures of transplantation experiments [192-197] detailed the conditions where transplantation was most appropriate, and concluded that transplantation should be viewed as a tool of last resort, for use only where natural recruitment and recovery processes are failing.

Simple, low-tech methods of coral transplantation have been investigated for restoring coral cover to damaged lower-energy reefs, using unattached coral fragments to mimic and accelerate asexual fragment-driven reef recovery processes [163-166, 198-200]. Transplanting corals into lower-energy areas precludes the necessity of securing coral transplants, thus considerably lowering cost and effort. A high survival rate for unattached coral transplants has been demonstrated for such sheltered areas [154, 163, 166, 198-201], particularly for rubble environments and for larger fragment sizes.

Transplants used as part of a community-based coral reef-management project. © The Coral Gardens Initiative.

Transplanting corals directly onto sand has also been done successfully [165, 200], establishing that entirely new patch reefs can be created on barren sand-flat 'deserts,' providing for increased fish habitat. The key factor in coral survival on sand is the large size of coral colonies, as small fragments always perish [200].

Coral Transplants as Fish Habitat; and Fish as Vital Component of Coral Reef Recovery

Living coral cover has been shown to positively influence fish abundance [202-205]. Certain species of reef fish are obligatory live-coral dwellers for life [204], while other species of reef fish require highly complex nocturnal or diurnal shelter provided by living corals [206]. If the lack of grazing fish is related to a lack of habitat, coral transplantation could potentially be important in re-establishing these fish populations, which would in turn clean the substratum and help re-establish a broader ecological balance [200]. However, if enough fish habitat remains on moderately degraded reefs, transplantation may not be required to restore the natural balance of fish to a reef, and fisheries management alone may lead to restoration.

Other types of ecological imbalances can inhibit reef recovery, and low-tech approaches to restoration are beginning to be investigated. Sea-urchin removal has proven effective in restoring corals to reefs with high post-recruitment mortality due to an over-abundance of bio-eroding sea urchins [207]. Crown-of-thorn starfish (COT) have also been removed from many reefs where COT over-abundance threatens coral population recovery. Reefs overgrown with macro-algae have also been restored by removing the algae, re-exposing coral recruitment surfaces [207].

Objectives

The primary objective of the ongoing work described here is to address the problem of delayed coral-reef resource recovery and the associated threat to the success of community-based no-take MPAs. The closure of reefs to fishing activities deprives communities of the use of portions of their fishing grounds. Severely degraded reefs low in fish habitat due to low coral cover and dominated by recruitment-inhibiting substrata, and missing breeding populations of formerly abundant organisms, may not respond effectively to closure, even after the conditions that lead to decline are discontinued. If a MPA is established by a community, and if the MPA takes many years to respond positively to closure, the delay would likely erode support for the project and cause the collapse of local management plans [208]. Active interventions, such as coral transplanting to increase fisheries habitat and restocking key shellfish species within the no-fishing MPAs, could potentially shorten the lag time in fisheries recovery, helping ensure the success of community-based management, and thus contributing significantly to coral-reef conservation. Simple, community-appropriate, and low-cost restoration methods, although still requiring further research to validate their successes, have recently been developed for use as workable tools for low-energy environments.

A secondary objective of the work is to increase community involvement and to raise awareness among the fishing communities for corals and other important reef species through hands-on restoration and restocking activities. Indeed, involving fishing communities in low-tech methods of coral transplantation could help to educate reef users about the importance of corals as fish habitat, how corals grow, and various environmental sensitivities of corals. Low-tech coral transplanting could thus potentially serve as a powerful hands-on educational tool in support of community-based management, even if implemented only on a relatively small-scale, and in association with community-managed marine reserves.

What Was Done

These methods are being used as part of a community-based coral reef-management project, The Coral Gardens Initiative, which is being implemented in the Pacific region by the Foundation for the Peoples of the South Pacific International (FSPI), in partnership with local FSPI affiliated NGOs. The initial sites (chosen as an ICRAN model site) are the eight coastal villages of Cuvu and Tuva Districts in Fiji. The project is being implemented in Fiji by FSP-Fiji, recently renamed Partners in Community Development Fiji. An ICRAN extension site is being established in the Solomon Islands, together with the FSPI affiliate, the Solomon Islands Development Trust. Recently obtained European Commission (EC) funding will allow for expansion to several other countries in the Pacific, and Counterpart International (the FSP-USA affiliate) is developing a planned Caribbean extension of the work.

Three basic types of coral-cover enhancement interventions are being used at the sites, each targeting a different habitat type: shallow-water high-energy reef flat areas; rubble-dominated lagoon areas resulting from dynamite fishing, coral harvesting, or severe storms; and sand-dominated 'lagoon deserts' where coral larvae cannot settle, but where corals grow well once established.

It is important to note that coral transplants should be obtained with minimal impact to healthy reefs. Rescuing jeopardized juvenile corals from extremely shallow reef areas before mortality events ensue (due to recurring disturbance [178, 209, 210]), and transplanting them into deeper reef areas, allows corals to survive and can provide a sustainable source for coral transplants [211]. Alternatively, coral fragments from fast-growing species can be taken for transplantation experiments to prevent competitive overgrowth and coral mortality. 'Coral gardening,' i.e. trimming overgrowing coral branches or replanting juvenile massive corals to appropriate restoration sites, offers promise as a means for obtaining coral transplants sustainably, while lowering the mortality of slower-growing corals on reefs, helping to increase reef biodiversity.

High Energy Reef Flats

At the main Fiji sites of Cuvu and Tuva districts, five MPAs were established in mid-2001 as part of a community-based plan to restore fisheries resources on rather severely degraded and over-fished reefs. The use of Derris plant poisons, although now effectively banned, was rampant at the start of the project. Nutrient pollution and siltation are also a problem at these sites due to proximity to a sugarcane growing and tourism-development area. In addition, chronic COT outbreaks and overgrowth by macro-algae appear to be related to land-based nutrification. Extreme temperatures and periodic storm wave assault are problematic to these fringing reef sites, so the restoration methods used for such degraded reef flats must resist waves and high temperatures. In these challenging sites, early coral transplanting experiments mostly failed, being destroyed by storm waves, killed due to temperature-induced bleaching, or by COT predation. However, in recent months, a major breakthrough in the methods has occurred, and restoration work is now focused on first constructing hollow, igloo-shaped, stone-and-cement 'fish houses'. These structures are about 40-50cm high and 40-50cm wide at the base, possess numerous holes to allow fish to enter for shelter, and have a larger hole at the top for later carrying (similar to the commercially available 'reef balls'). After being cured for 2-3 days under damp sand until hard (avoiding contact with salt water), each fish house was carried on a bamboo pole to the shore and carried or transported by canoe to the deployment areas on the reef flat. The fish houses were cemented to the reef base in tide pools on the reef flats with cement mixed with fresh water. After securing, these multi-windowed fish houses, situated above the often-shifting reef debris, serve as stable bases for planting corals and restocking Tridacnid clams. In these sites, increased fish numbers, probably due to increased habitat (and MPA establishment), seem to have led to a reduction in algal overgrowth.

Within the Fiji MPAs, 500 Tridacnid clams of three species, obtained from the Department of Fisheries clam hatchery, have been restocked. Close to 1,000 Trochus, 1,500 Turbo, 2,000 chitons, 2,000 Anadara clams, and 50 Lambis spider conch, obtained from women fishers in Rewa province, were also restocked into appropriate habitats. Predatory snails among the Tridacna clams and strong storm waves have caused relatively severe clam losses. However, clams placed directly onto the fish houses five days before the storm were not swept away. In addition, these clams, being elevated above the substratum, appear to suffer less from snail predation. Juvenile Trochus have been observed in abundance inside fish house structures and appear to prefer such cryptic habitat. While these sorts of results can at best be considered preliminary, they indicate a potential for enhancement of reef-restocking areas to conform to the conditions of the particular reef area.

Rubble Dominated Areas

Rubble beds dominate the lagoons of Malaita, Solomon Islands. They are the result of generations of coral harvesting to produce betel-nut lime and to use as fill material to construct 'artificial islands' in the lagoons, as well as a recent upsurge in dynamite fishing. Where reefs have been converted into shifting gravel-sized rubble, coral larvae can still recruit, but often fail to develop past recruitment stages. At these sites, restoration can be a rather simple process, simply scattering coral branches of various sizes into small test patches, and expanding the work (or not) based on obtained results. 'Staghorn' *Acropora* corals have worked well due to their rapid growth and ability to reattach to and re-cement rubble. *Porites* corals, although growing considerably slower, tend to work better in silty areas or areas with periodic freshwater runoff. Coral branches over 15cm tend to be more successful than smaller sizes. The next phase of the Solomon Islands lagoon restoration work will involve training coral harvesters in sustainable coral farming techniques to replace wild coral harvesting.

Sand Dominated Sites

Sheltered lagoon areas of barren sand are also being enhanced, particularly at Marau Sound, Solomon Islands, by transplanting coral colonies directly onto the sand. Small fragments often die due to close contact with the sand, thus only highly branched and larger colonies are used, often taken from corals grown in the rubble restoration sites. Isolated patch reefs created this way, particularly coral colonies planted further away (>50m) from the reef, serve as nursery habitat for fish recruiting from planktonic larval stages [200].

For future work, coral colonies for use in transplanting on sand can be grown in about 2-3 years from smaller fragments scattered on rubble beds [165].

Self-assessment of Success in Achieving the Objectives to Date

So far, 150 of the fish-house structures have been made by community fish wardens, and about 130 have thus far been deployed at Yanuca Island. One additional site, several kilometres away at Yadua village, is also being set up. The corals are doing exceptionally well, and of hundreds of transplanted colonies, no mortality has been observed. Storm waves hit the site in July, and while they shattered and threw unattached natural coral colonies onto the shore, they caused no damage to the corals transplanted onto the ten fish house structures that had been deployed at the time. COT occasionally must be removed (about seven so far), and these pest species have caused partial mortality of several colonies.

A wide diversity of colourful fish has moved into the corals at all Solomons and Fiji sites, and experimental areas have become popular tourist attractions at the Fiji's Shangri-La Resort and Marau Sound's Tavanipupu Resort. This is an added benefit to the work, and as a result these resorts have been major financial and in-kind contributors in both countries.

Adaptation of shores to increasing waves (potentially in part due to climate change) is also being studied in the experiment, as storm and tsunami waves are frequent in this particular coastal area. The fish house structures are full of holes, have a high surface area, and as they are about 40 cm above the reef base, give a higher profile to the otherwise very flat inner reef, intercepting wave energy and allowing it to dissipate within the structure. Storm run-up onto the adjacent shore will be measured in areas with and without fish house structures to assess their effectiveness during storms, and differences in beach erosion/accretion will be noted.

The transplantation of corals more tolerant to heat stress may also have implications in helping reefs adapt to climate change, but this work is still in its early stages and may need more extensive and detailed scientific monitoring than the community is capable of at this point.

Recommendations

Before widespread transplantation is attempted at any specific site, transplantation trials using diverse fragments and species should be carried out and observed for at least a year to determine feasibility: site suitability, relative fragment mortality, and possible methods modifications required to increase success.

It is important to include as diverse an assortment of coral transplants as is practical in the sites, understanding that corals less suited to the particular site will eventually die out. Coral reef restoration sites including as much species diversity and within-species clonal diversity as possible will help ensure resilience of the coral population to changing environmental conditions, and provide for greater disease resistance, as well as greater spawning compatibility.

Because massive coral species grow considerably slower than branching corals, they generally have been neglected in coral reef restoration research. The establishment of massive corals in transplantation sites where their survival over time is likely could have long-lasting positive impacts, as these corals live for centuries and survive severe storms, while branching species are more ephemeral, being easily killed or swept away.

More work is needed to refine the methods further, with more statistical verification that the work is helping with MPA recovery. Much of the work should therefore be considered preliminary in nature. There is a need for more in-depth study of all aspects of coral transplantation for reef restoration presented here.

Limitations and Potentials of Coral Transplanting for Reef Restoration

Severely degraded reefs chronically impacted by siltation, pollution, or ongoing destructive fishing will not recover coral populations naturally [209], and transplantation cannot be expected to restore corals to such chronically disturbed reefs, as long as conditions causing coral mortality continue.

If natural processes of larval recruitment and fragmentation lead to recovery of coral populations without intervention, restoration efforts involving transplantation are not required [187, 200]. Discontinuing negative impacts on coral reefs alone may often be sufficient for the recovery of some reefs. On such reefs, coral transplantation may be contraindicated, as coral transplants could potentially overgrow and kill diverse natural coral recruits.

A Precautionary Approach to Coral Manipulations

Coral-reef restoration methods that involve species manipulations and transplanting corals could also have unforeseen consequences to the basic ecology of partially intact reef systems, or could degrade or alter donor reefs, and thus monitoring and a precautionary approach is required. The unwise application of coral transplantation might favour unnatural species compositions and distributions and could cause the demise of particular species. For example, staghorn species of *Acropora* spp. have the ability to out-compete slower-growing and long-lived massive corals, and these massive corals are more resistant to cyclones, and might also be more tolerant of temperature and salinity extremes. Indiscriminate transplanting of *Acropora* spp. could lower overall coral diversity on reefs and could make reefs more vulnerable to disturbance.

Transplanting corals for coral-reef restoration should by no means be regarded as a universal solution for the dire position coral reefs are facing today. Prevention of coral-reef decline is a considerably more effective management strategy than restoration. If the limited effectiveness of coral-reef restoration is not fully appreciated, especially by the press, restoration efforts might give a false sense of hope, dissipating the sense of urgency for coral-reef conservation.

LESSONS LEARNED

Stakeholder Involvement and Community Support

- Involving community members in coral transplantation work helps to build a deeper understanding and appreciation for corals as fish habitat as well as their biological requirements.

- Coral transplantation *may* help accelerate reef recovery and thus benefits accruing to communities from a MPA, in turn sustaining support for resource management.

Sustainable Management of Resources

- Restoration work is only to be used in areas where a ban on the use of destructive fishing practices has been successfully implemented and enforced, and MPAs are effectively and permanently closed to fishing.

- Severely degraded reefs chronically impacted by siltation or pollution will not recover coral populations naturally, and transplantation cannot be expected to restore corals to such disturbed reefs as long as conditions causing coral mortality continue.

- Restoration work should NOT be undertaken if natural processes of larval recruitment and fragmentation lead to recovery of coral populations without interventions.

- Small trials should always be run first in new areas to test for restoration success.

- Transplanting corals should not be regarded as a universal solution to coral reef decline. Prevention of the latter is a considerably more effective management strategy than restoration.

- Caution is to be used in all experiments, and it is important to remember that results are likely to be site and species-specific.

- Incorporating diversity into restoration experiments and adapting methods through trial and error is vital.

- Coral transplants should be obtained from areas where their survival is jeopardized. Alternatively, fragments from fast-growing species may be used for transplantation purposes.

- The construction of 'fish houses' may allow for more rapid recovery of corals, Tridacnids, and trochus in high-energy reef flats.

- It is important to note that reef-restoration methods are preliminary in nature.

Capacity Building; Public Awareness and Education

- Coral transplantation is a good educational tool.

- Where restoration work is being carried out to rehabilitate reefs damaged due to destructive fishing methods, awareness-raising and education programmes of community members in the use of sustainable harvest techniques have to complement restoration activities.

Monitoring

- Restoration may have unforeseen consequences, and thus, to ensure transplantation success, monitoring and a precautionary approach are required.

- Transplantation success will also depend on the implementation of other types of community-based interventions, such as COT starfish removal.

PART XIII
CONCLUSIONS AND RECOMMENDATIONS

The case studies presented in this publication vary substantially in the context and factors that affect management of Marine Protected Areas (MPAs). Although generalizations are always difficult to make, there are some common threads of success and challenges that may help us in implementing MPAs at new locations, and refining management at existing ones.

The challenges that MPAs address are remarkably consistent across a large range of societal and geographical settings. They generally include:

- Degradation of coastal ecosystems and associated loss in biodiversity.

- Overexploitation of natural resources.

- Unsustainable development and land use practices.

- Increased conflicts over access rights between individual user groups.

In attempting to address and mitigate those issues, many of the unsuccessful MPAs have been those that have not received community and stakeholder support. The management of these reserves has tended to underestimate or ignore the social and economic importance of the areas for its users, who have, in turn, ignored the protected area designation. As stated in the United Nations Conference on the Environment and Development (UNCED, 1992) Agenda 21, if Integrated Coastal Zone Management (ICZM) and MPAs are to be successfully implemented, then all concerned individuals need to be and feel empowered at the relevant (local) level. This recognition has led to the strong emphasis on developing community-based management of tropical coastal environments. However, increasing stakeholder support and participation in park management does not necessarily diminish the role of government.

Designing a governance framework which allows for natural resources to be managed sustainably involves strategies to instil and invest appropriate responsibility in the primary stakeholders, whilst responsibility for overall policy and coordination of functions might continue to lie with a level of government. Governments often play a unique role in sustainable resource management projects by providing, for example, financial and technical assistance as well as policy and legislative support. This assistance and support often increases the legitimacy and accountability of community-based systems by creating co-management arrangements. However, legislation, policies, and good intentions do not guarantee that coastal and marine resources will be used sustainably. Education, public outreach and the building of a constituency are vital for all stakeholders to understand and appreciate the issues and factors involved in coastal zone management. The establishment of such participatory arrangements may often represent a major 'cultural' change from past experiences, requiring time, patience, and a continual process of confidence building, flexibility, open dialogue, and commitment.

Although help from international organizations in the form, for example, of seed money and provision of human capacity can be instrumental in paving the road to success for a MPA, project ownership must lie with local stakeholders if sustainable and effective management is to be maintained. The establishment of technical advisory committees, with delegates from all stakeholder groups equitably represented, is often key in creating win-win situations and developing sustainable management strategies. Technical advisory boards also offer stakeholders the opportunity to collaborate with government departments to access international funding. When developing working relationships among participants, it is critical to build trust and an atmosphere of compromise, as they are often necessary to overcome conflict situations (which generally are dynamic and evolving) and reach consensus. Analysis and debates of issues at stake should occur during regular meetings. It is important to note that at times small, focused meetings, involving only a subset of all participants may be crucial in obtaining the views, insights and aspirations of stakeholder groups or subgroups (e.g., women, marginal ethnic populations) that may be reluctant to participate actively in large or mixed groups.

In order to conserve and protect biodiversity, in a framework where people and development also have a place, practical management plans need to be drafted that include zoning, stakeholder involvement and watersheds. MPAs management often focuses on the marine component of the coast, often leaving watershed inadequately addressed. However, effective ICZM involves also managing adjacent terrestrial areas in order to minimize impacts from poor land-use and development practices. Strict management oversight and control of development on coastal areas should be enforced and new developments should be required to have formulated Environmental Impact Assessments (EIA) prior to construction and follow advice arising from them.

To formulate a feasible management plan, reliable baseline data, regular assessments and monitoring of coral reefs and environmental resources are required. These activities: (i) illustrate to coastal communities the condition of their environment, (ii) encourage and foster their participation in management and (iii) allow quantifiable measurements of the effects of protection on the resource base. In addition to ecological data, socio-economic information should also be recorded, following standard protocols to allow for comparisons over time and space. Such monitoring activities typically require simple materials and can be easily implemented using park rangers and/or other park staff. Here again, to be successful in their implementation, it is essential that such plans be 'owned' and understood by all relevant local members. Thus, it is important to understand the capacity of individual stakeholder groups, develop an atmosphere where these groups feel comfortable to voice questions and comments, and adjust development and pace of management plan design accordingly. Slight delays in implementation at the start, to accommodate varying capacity levels amongst members, are often worthwhile to ensure long-term sustainability. In such a context, the use of non-culture specific tools (e.g., buoys in Banco Chinchorro, Mexico) proves valuable in facilitating common understanding.

In order to gain consensus on a General Management Plan, education and public-awareness campaigns often prove essential. Not only do they help promote (i) sustainable fishing and resources-use methods by allowing fishermen to gain a basic understanding of the biological aspects of the resources they harvest and the true impact of destructive fishing methods, but also (ii) a broad-level understanding of the complexity of ecological systems, and thus importance of sustainably managing them. Finally, regular reviews of a reserve management plan, highlighting its strengths and weaknesses, can help formulate a more efficient and effective management structure. MPA management is iterative, adaptive, and requires continuous learning. All concerns cannot necessarily be addressed at once and, hence, some issues will need to be prioritized. Moreover, the management process needs to be flexible in order to adapt to arising pressures and opportunities.

Management plans will also have to address issues of important and fragile ecosystem protection and balance these needs with 'sustainable use'. MPAs that advocate and allow for multiple uses reflect this understanding. A zoning plan is a useful and important tool in mitigating between stakeholders, clarifying temporal and spatial resource-use and separating incompatible activities to avoid or limit conflicts. Such management plans should protect sensitive habitats and ban extractive and damaging activities from such areas (essentially no-take) and confine intensive use to areas that are able to withstand it. Zoning patterns should be as simple as possible and visibly delineated, while user-rules should be clearly defined and effectively communicated to all stakeholders. Moreover, the zoning pattern should be the result of a participatory and collaborative process, involving all stakeholders (primary as well as secondary), that is open to negotiation and where conflicting user-groups are willing to accept some compromises.

Similarly, it is vital to address displacement of stakeholder activities through the protection of resources for conservation initiatives. Alternative livelihoods should be researched and tested for their viability and suitability to the area and for the local community, and integrated into the management plan from the very start of MPA planning.

Ultimately, an *enforced* regulatory/legal framework is essential in order for MPA management to be successful. Without enforcement, cohesiveness of stakeholder groups is likely to break down, distrust may settle in, open conflicts emerge, and all initial efforts to bring about sustainable utilization of resources are at risk of being nullified. Thus, it is critical that consensus of objectives be established as it brings about legitimacy of regulations and their enforcement; i.e. it is essential to instil a sense of ownership of local resources in the park's main stakeholders. Enforcement activities are likely to be most effective if public participation is encouraged and such initiatives seconded by local governmental institutions, thus strengthening surveillance capacity within MPAs through institutional arrangements. NGOs and other partnerships can act as important catalysts for increasing capacity for management and enforcement. Punishment should fit the crime, i.e. fines should act as true deterrents; sanctions should be graduated (increase for repeat offenders) and context-dependent (e.g., subsistence poaching v. commercial poaching). As highlighted in the development of management plans, success is most likely to be achieved by strengthening education programmes to improve and discuss acceptance of regulations and compliance levels, as well as promote peer-enforcement of rules. Easily identifiable zoning boundaries as well as clear user rules are important elements in facilitating and helping to warrant enforcement.

While the development of most sustainable management initiatives will require initial financial support in the form of grants, seed money and/or technical support, stakeholders should aspire to develop financially self-sufficient MPAs. Indeed, enforcement and monitoring programmes are long-term initiatives, requiring the establishment of long -term 'working relationships' and 'administrative structures' as well as funding. At the same time donors must recognise and support 'less glamorous' but ultimately essential management activities for reserves (e.g. enforcement). Public–private partnerships can play an important role in helping to increase awareness and capacity for management, as well as develop sustainable financing mechanisms. However, it is important to remember that management processes should balance the needs and interests of all stakeholder groups. One of the most popular and successful mechanisms advocated for establishing financial independence, is the implementation of user fees, as long as these are clearly earmarked for conservation. Administration of funds should also be transparent and involve the participation of stakeholders.

Support for MPAs extends beyond the financial realm, with public awareness, capacity building and education representing some of the most important and effective management strategies aimed at protecting reef environments. To strengthen capacity building, information gained should be adequately documented and made publicly available; such outreach can increase awareness about existing successes, lessons learned, and remaining challenges, and allows effective initiatives to be replicated at other sites in other countries and/or regions. Education and capacity building programmes should help identify, assess, publicize and develop or adapt research outputs, training manuals and successful case studies. Moreover, attendance at local, regional and international meetings helps foster information exchange between managers and practitioners and develop collaborative initiatives. There is much to learn from others' experiences, in particular how different issues have been approached in a variety of settings. Sharing knowledge, transferring lessons learned, meeting others who have undergone similar difficulties, and/or celebrated comparable successes, are important in maintaining involvement, and ensuring long-term commitment.

Given the increasing number of projects developing tools and activities related to sustainable management of coastal and marine resources, and to sustain efforts over time (at the national, regional and international level), it will be key to develop indicators of success, both in terms of improvements in ecological parameters and socio-economic gains, as well as perform regular evaluations of active programmes.

PART X
REFERENCES

1.   Jameson SC, JW McManus, and MD Spalding 1995. *State of the reefs: regional and global perspectives*. NOAA: Washington DC, USA. ICRI Executive Secretariat Background Paper. pp 32

2.   Spalding MD, C Ravilious, and EP Green 2001. *World Atlas of Coral Reefs*. University of California Press: Berkeley, USA

3.   Groombridge B and MD Jenkins 2002. *World Atlas of Biodiversity*. University of California Press: Berkeley, USA

4.   ICRAN 2002. *Coral Reef Action – Sustaining Communities Worldwide*. ICRAN: Cambridge, UK. pp 15

5.   United Nations 2002. *Report of the World Summit on Sustainable Development Johannesburg, South Africa, 26 August-4 September 2002*. United Nations: New York, USA. Number A/CONF.199/20

6.   ICRAN. *International Coral Reef Action Network*. http://coral.unep.ch/icrantype2.htm (Accessed December 29, 2003)

7.   Burke L, L Selig, and M Spalding 2002. *Reefs at Risk in Southeast Asia*. World Resource Institute: Washington DC, USA.

8.   ICRAN 2003. *International Tropical Ecosystems Management Symposium ITMEMS 2. Workshop Summary: Role of Marine Protected Areas in Management – ICRAN Session*. pp 7

9.   Dight IJ and LM Scherl 1997. The International Coral Reef Initiative (ICRI): Global priorities for the conservation and management of coral reefs and the need for partnerships. *Coral Reefs Supplement*, **6**: S139-S147

10.   UNEP. *International Coral Reef Action network (ICRAN) – Caribbean Region*. http://www.cep.unep.org/programmes/spaw/icran/icran.htm (Accessed December 12, 2003)

11.   UNEP 2002. *Report of the Meeting of the Regional Group of Experts on the International Coral Reef Action Network*. In Proceedings of the Meeting of the Regional Group of Experts on the International Coral Reef Action Network. Phuket, Thailand

12.   WRI. http://www.wri.org/wri/reefsatrisk/ (Accessed December 29, 2003)

13.   Adler 2003. A world of neighbours: UNEP's Regional Seas Programme. *Tropical Coasts*: 12-18

14.   UNEP. *Regional Seas*. http://www.unep.ch/seas/ (Accessed January 24, 2004)

15.   UNEP. *Regional Seas: joining hands around the seas*. http://www.unep.ch/seas/main/hoverv.html (Accessed December 12, 2003)

16.   UNEP 1982. *UNEP: Guidelines and principles for the preparation and implementation of comprehensive action plans for the protection and development of marine and coastal areas of Regional Seas*. UNEP. UNEP Regional Seas Reports and Studies, Number 15. pp 11

17.   UNEP 1984. *UNEP: UNEP Regional Seas Programme: the Eastern African experience*. UNEP. UNEP Regional Seas Reports and Studies, Number 53. pp 15

18.   UNEP Regional Seas. *Regional Seas Programme*. http://www.unep.org/unep/program/natres/water/regseas/regseas.htm#_actionplan (Accessed January 9, 2004)

19.   CEP-UNEP. *Assessment and Management of Environmental Pollution (AMEP)*. http://www.cep.unep.org/who/amep.htm (Accessed January 12, 2004)

20.   GPA. *East Asian Seas*. http://www.gpa.unep.org/seas/workshop/EASIAN.htm (Accessed January 10, 2004)

21.   Smith D 2004. personal communication

22.   Salmona P 2002. The regional seas in the 21st century: the need for data. *Ocean and Coastal management*, **45**: 935-964

23.   UNEP Regional Seas. *Regional Seas Conventions and Protocols*. http://www.unep.ch/seas/main/hconlist.html (Accessed June 1, 2004)

24.   GPA. *Eastern African Region*. http://www.gpa.unep.org/seas/workshop/EAFRICAN.htm (Accessed January 10, 2004)

25.   UNEP 2001. *Opportunities and Challenges for Coordination between Marine and Regional Fishery Bodies and Regional Seas Conventions*. Regional Seas Reports and Studies, Number 175

26.   GPA. *ROPME Sea Region*. http://www.gpa.unep.org/seas/workshop/ROPME.htm (Accessed January 10, 2004)

27.   UNEP Regional Seas 1991. *UNEP Regional Seas Reports and Studies No. 135, 1991*. www.unep.ch/seas/Archive/rsrs135.html (Accessed January 9, 2004)

PART X

28. GPA. *North East Pacific.* http://www.gpa.unep.org/seas/workshop/NEP.htm (Accessed January 10, 2004)

29. UNEP. *North-East Pacific Convention adopted.* http://www.unep.ch/seas/main/news/nepnews.html (Accessed January 10, 2004)

30. GPA. *North West Pacific (NOWPAP).* http://www.gpa.unep.org/seas/workshop/NWPAC.htm (Accessed January 10, 2004)

31. GPA. *Red Sea and Gulf of Aden.* http://www.gpa.unep.org/seas/workshop/REDSEA.htm (Accessed January 10, 2004)

32. GPA. *South East Pacific Region.* http://www.gpa.unep.org/seas/workshop/SEPAC.htm (Accessed January 10, 2004)

33. GPA. *South West Atlantic Region.* http://www.gpa.unep.org/seas/workshop/SWATLAN.htm (Accessed January 10, 2004)

34. GPA. *West and Central African Region.* http://www.gpa.unep.org/seas/workshop/WACAF.htm (Accessed January 10, 2004)

35. UNEP 1991. *Regional Seas Programme of UNEP.* UNEP Regional Seas. UNEP Regional Seas Reports and Studies, Number 135. pp 45

36. UNEP 2000. *Regional Seas: A Survival Strategy for our Oceans and Coasts.* UNEP. pp 24

37. ICRI. *International Coral Reef Initiative Events Detail. ITMEMS 2.* http://www.icriforum.org/router.cfm?show=event_detail.cfm?CID=87 (Accessed December 10, 2003)

38. Anonymous. *GDP, population, exports and imports of ACS countries.* www.acs-aec.org/Trade/DBase/DBase_eng/dbaseindex_eng.htm (Accessed June 1, 2004)

39. UNEP Caribbean Environment Programme 1989. *Regional Overview of Environmental Problems and Priorities Affecting the Coastal and Marine Resources of the Wider Caribbean Region.* CEP-UNEP. CEP Technical Report, Number 2

40. GPA. *Wider Caribbean Region.* http://www.gpa.unep.org/seas/workshop/CARIB.htm (Accessed January 10, 2004)

41. Linton D, R Smith, P Alcolado, C Hanson, P Edwards, R Estrada, T Fisher, R Gomez Fernandez, F Geraldes, C McCoy, D Vaughan, V Voegeli, G Warner, and J Wiener 2002. Status of coral reefs in the northern Caribbean and Atlantic node of the GCRMN, In: *Status of Coral Reefs of the World: 2002,* by C Wilkinson (ed). Australian Institute of Marine Science: Townsville, Australia. pp 277-300

42. Almada-Villela P, M McField, P Kramer, P Richards Kramer, and E Arias-Gonzalez 2002. Status of coral reefs of Mesoamerica – Mexico, Belize, Guatemala, Honduras, Nicaragua and El Salvador, In: *Status of Coral Reefs of the World,* by C Wilkinson (ed). Australian Institute of Marine Science: Townsville, Australia. pp 303-321

43. Miller MAL 1996. Protecting the Marine Environment of the Wider Caribbean Region: the Challenge of Institution Building, In: *Green Globe Yearbook.* pp 37-46

44. Andrade Colmenares N. *Caribbean Action Plan: embracing diversity.* www.unep.ch/seas/carcap.html (Accessed January 13, 2004)

45. Hoetjes P, A Lum Kong, R Juman, A Miller, M Miller, K De Meyer, and A Smith 2002. Status of coral reefs in the Eastern Caribbean: the OECS, Trinidad and Tobago, Barbados and the Netherland Antilles, In: *Status of Coral Reefs of the World: 2002,* by C Wilkinson (ed). Australian Institute of Marine Science: Townsville, Australia. pp 325-337

46. UNEP World Conservation Monitoring Centre 2002. *Recreation and Tourism.* http://www.oceanatlas.org/servlet/CDSServlet?status=ND0xODU2Jjc9ZW4mNjE9Y3RuJjY1PWluZm8~ (Accessed January 10, 2004)

47. CEP-UNEP 1996. *Common Guidelines and Criteria for Protected Areas in the Wider Caribbean region: Identification, Selection, Establishment and Management.* CEP-UNEP. CEP Technical Report, Number 37

48. UNEP 1997. *Coastal Tourism in the Wider Caribbean Region: Impacts and Best management Practices.* UNEP Caribbean Environment Programme: Kingston, Jamaica. CEP Technical Report, Number 38. pp 85

49. CEP-UNEP. *Specially Protected Areas and Wildlife (SPAW).* http://www.cep.unep.org/who/spaw.htm (Accessed January 12, 2004)

50. CEP-UNEP. *Education, Training and Awareness (ETA).* http://www.cep.unep.org/who/eta.htm (Accessed January 12, 2004)

51. CEP-UNEP. *Information Systems for the Management of Marine and Coastal Resources (CEPNET).* http://www.cep.unep.org/who/cepnet.htm (Accessed January 12, 2004)

52. Burke L 2002. Reefs at Risk in the Caribbean, In: *Status of Coral Reefs of the World: 2002*, by C Wilkinson (ed). Australian Institute of Marine Science: Townsville, Australia. p 324

53. UNESCO. *Sian Ka'an*. http://whc.unesco.org/sites/410.htm (Accessed January 2, 2004)

54. UNEP World Conservation Monitoring Centre. *World Heritage Sites.* http://www.wcmc.org.uk/protected_areas/data/wh/sianka'a.html (Accessed January 24, 2004)

55. NOAA. *Sian Ka'an Biosphere Reserve, Mexico.* http://effectivempa.noaa.gov/sites/siankaan.html (Accessed January 24, 2004)

56. NOAA. *Banco Chinchorro Biosphere Reserve (RBBCH), Mexico.* http://effectivempa.noaa.gov/sites/chinchorro.html (Accessed January 24, 2004)

57. ICRI. *Banco Chinchorro Biosphere Reserve (Mexico).* http://www.icriforum.org/router.cfm?show=secretariat/good_practices.html&Item=8 (Accessed January 24, 2004)

58. ICRAN. *Bonaire Marine Park.* http://www.icran.org/SITES/doc/bmp.pdf (Accessed January 15, 2004)

59. ICRAN 2002. Bonaire National Marine Park, Netherlands Antilles – ICRAN Demonstration Site, In: *Status of Coral Reefs of the World: 2002*, by C Wilkinson (ed). Australian Institute of Marine Science: Townsville, Australia. pp 338-339

60. Scura L and T van't Hof 1993. *The ecology and economics of Bonaire Marine Park.* The World Bank: Washington DC. The World Bank Environment Department Divisional Paper, Number 1993-44

61. De Meyer K 1994. *Sustainable tourism?* In Developing Ecotourism: balancing dollars and sense. Proceedings of the 4th Caribbean Conference on Ecotourism. Bonaire, Dutch Antilles

62. De Meyer K 1997. How tourism can help protect the environment: a case study of the Bonaire Marine Park. *UNEP Industry and Environment*, Oct-Dec (Tourism focus)

63. De Meyer K 1997. *Marine environment and tourism: maximum ten divers per square meter.* In Proceedings of the Conference on Sustainable Tourism for the Netherland Antilles. St Marteen, Dutch Caribbean

64. De Meyer K 1998. Bonaire: Netherland Antilles, In: *Caribbean Coral Reef, Seagrass and Mangrove Sites*, by B Kjerfve (ed). UNESCO

65. De Meyer K 1998. *Making tourism work for the Bonaire Marine Park.* In Proceedings of the ITMEMS. Townsville, Australia. pp 251-252

66. De Meyer K 1999. *1999 and beyond: Management strategy and action plan.* Bonaire Marine Park.

67. Dixon J and PB Sherman 1990. *Economics of Protected Areas: A new look at benefits and costs.* East West Centre, Island Press

68. Dixon J 1993. Economic benefits of Marine Protected Areas. *Oceanus*, **36**(3): 35-40

69. Dixon J, L Scura, and T van't Hof 1993. Meeting ecological and economic goals: Marine parks in the Caribbean. *Ambio*, **22**(3-3): 117-125

70. van't Hof T 1992. Bonaire Marine Park: the story behind success. *Ocean Realm*, December Issue

71. ICRAN 2002. Soufriere Management Area, St Lucia, In: *Status of Coral reefs of the World*, by C Wilkinson (ed). Australian Institute of Marine Science: Townsville, Australia. p 340

72. ICRAN. *Soufriere Marine Management Area – SMMA.* www.icran.org (Accessed December 15, 2003)

73. Government of Saint Lucia (GOSL) Statistical Department 2001. personal communication

74. Department of Fisheries (DOF) Data Management Section 2001. personal communication

75. Sandersen H and S Koester 2000. Co-management of tropical coastal zones: the case of the Soufriere Marine Management Area, Saint Lucia, W.I. *Coastal Management*, **28**: 87-97

76. George S 1996. *A Review of the Creation, Implementation and Initial Operation of the Soufriere Marine Management Area.* Department of Fisheries: Castries, Saint Lucia. pp 17

77. SMMA 1998. *Conflict Resolution and Participatory Planning: The Case of the Soufriere Marine Management Area.* Soufriere, St Lucia. pp 14

78. Pierre D 2000. Adjusting to a new way of life: marine management areas and fishers. *The OECS Fisher*, A Special Fisheries Publication of the Organisation of Eastern Caribbean States/Natural Resources Management Unit: 22-27

79. SRDF 1994. *Soufriere Marine Management Area: Agreement on the Use and Management of Marine and Coastal Resources in the Soufriere Region, St Lucia.* SRDF in collaboration with the Caribbean Natural Resources Institute and the Department of Fisheries. pp 25

80. Dahl C 1997. Integrated coastal resources management and community participation in a small island setting. *Ocean and Coastal management*, **36**(1-3): 23-45

81. Rivera R and GF Newkirk 1997. Power from the people: a documentation of non-governmental organizations' experience in community-based coastal resource management in the Philippines. *Ocean and Coastal management*, **36**(1-3): 73-75

82. Brown N 1997. *Devolution of Authority over the Management of Natural Resources: The Soufriere Marine Management Area, Saint Lucia.* Prepared by the Caribbean Natural Resources Institute for the Caribbean Centre for Development Administration under UNDP. Caribbean Capacity 21 Project

83. Renard Y 1998. *Integrated coastal zone management: the role of civil society.* OAS Coastal Zone Management Project. Discussion Papers for Natural Resources Management in the Caribbean. pp 12-17

84. Pierre D. 1999 1999. *The Soufriere Marine Management Area.* In Proceedings of the Workshop on Ecological and Social Impacts in Planning Caribbean Marine Reserves. Montego Bay, Jamaica

85. Salm R, J Clark, and E Siirila 2000. *Marine and Coastal Protected Areas: A Guide for Planners and Managers.* International Union for the Conservation of Nature and Natural Resources. pp 370

86. Roberts C, M Nugues, and J Hawkins 1997. *Report of the 1997 Survey of Coral Reefs of the Soufriere Marine Management Area and Anse la Raye, Saint Lucia.* UK Darwin Initiative and Natural Environment Research Council. pp 13

87. Gell F, C Roberts, and R Goodridge 2001. *The Fishery Effects of the Soufriere Marine Management Area 1995/6 to 2000/1.* UK Darwin Initiative; Natural Environment Research Council; The Pew Charitable Trust; UK Department of International Development. pp 77

88. SMMA 1999. *Agreement to Manage the Soufriere Marine Management Area.* Soufriere, Saint Lucia. pp 7

89. SMMA 1999. *Draft Bylaw No 1 relating to the conduct of the Soufriere Marine Management Associations as a not-for-profit-company under the 1996 Company's Act of Saint Lucia.*

90. Linton D 2003. *Proposal to ICRI Small-Scale Development Projects. Monitoring of Status of Coral Reefs in the Portland Bight Protected Area (PBPA) of Jamaica.* pp 5

91. PBPA. *Human Population.* http://www.portlandbight.com.jm/humanpop.htm (Accessed January 27, 2004)

92. PBPA. *Marine Life in the PBPA.* http://www.portlandbight.com.jm/Marine.html (Accessed January 27, 2004)

93. PBPA. http://www.portlandbight.com.jm/manobject.htm (Accessed January 27, 2004)

94. Hayton S and H Grabowsky 2001. *Buccoo Reef Marine Park.* http://www.scsoft.de/et/et2.nsf/0/E1F92F5876B22368C1256307007B8180?OpenDocument (Accessed 30 January, 2004)

95. Brown K, WN Adger, E Tompkins, P Bacon, D Shim, and K Young 2001. Trade-off analysis for marine protected area management. *Ecological Economics*, **37**: 417-434

96. Anonymous. *Consensus building in the Caribbean.* New Agriculturist Online. http://www.new-agri.co.uk/01-1/develop/dev03.html (Accessed June 3, 2004)

97. Francis J, A Nilsson, and D Waruinge 2002. Marine Protected Areas in the Eastern African Region: how successful are they? *Ambio*, **31**(7-8): 503-511

98. Obura D, L Celliers, H Machano, S Mangubhai, MS Mohammed, H Motta, C Muhando, N Muthiga, M Pereira, and M Schleyer 2002. Status of coral reefs in Eastern Africa: Kenya, Tanzania, Mozambique and South Africa, In: *Status of Coral Reefs of the World: 2002*, by C Wilkinson (ed). Australian Institute of Marine Science: Townsville, Australia. pp 63-78

99. Linden O and CG Lundin 1996. *The journey from Arusha to Seychelles.* In Proceedings of the Second Policy Conference on Integrated Coastal Management in Eastern Africa and Island States. Successes and failures in integrated coastal zone management in Eastern Africa and Island States. Seychelles. World Bank, Environment Department; SIDA, Department for research and Cooperation, SAREC

100. Ahamada S, L Bigot, J Bijoux, J Maharavo, S Meunier, M Moyne-Picard, and N Paupiah 2002. Status of coral reefs in the South West Indian Island Node: Comoros, Madagascar, Mauritius, Reunion and Seychelles, In: *Status of Coral Reefs of the World: 2002*, by C Wilkinson (ed). Australian Institute of Marine Science: Townsville, Australia. pp 79-100

101. Lundin CG and O Linden 1995. *Integrated Coastal Zone Management in the Seychelles.* In Proceedings of the National Workshop on Integrated Coastal Zone Management in the Seychelles. Seychelles. The World Bank, Environment Department; SIDA, Department for Research Cooperation, SAREC

102. Muhando C and J Francis 2000. *The status of coral reefs in the Dar es Salaam Marine Reserves system and the state of reefs in other marine protected areas of Tanzania.* Institute of Marine Science (IMS): Zanzibar.

103. Muhando CA and MS Mohammed 2002. Coral reef benthos and fisheries in Tanzania before and after the 1998 bleaching and mortality event. *Western Indian Ocean Journal of Marine Sciences*, **1**(1): 43-52

104. ICRAN 2002. Malindi and Watamu National Park and Reserve, Kenya – ICRAN Demonstration Site, In: *Status of Coral Reefs of the World: 2002*, by C Wilkinson (ed). Australian Institute of Marine Science: Townsville, Australia. p 74

105. Perry CT 2003. Reef development at Inhaca Island, Mozambique: Coral communities and impacts of the 1999/2000 Southern African floods. *Ambio*, **32**(2): 134-139

106. NOAA 2004. *National Environmental Satellite, Data, and Information Service. Coral bleaching reports.* http://orbit-net.nesdis.noaa.gov/orad/sub/bleaching_report_index.html (Accessed January 29, 2004)

107. Bryant P 2003. *South Africa and Mozambique Announce Important New Marine Protected Areas.* http://www.wwf.dk/4402774 (Accessed January 29, 2004)

108. UNEP. *Regional Seas Programme for Eastern Africa. Overview.* http://www.unep.ch/seas/main/eaf/eafover.html (Accessed May 21, 2004)

109. UNEP. *Regional Seas Directory.* http://www.oilandgasforum.net/regional_forums/regdir.htm (Accessed May 21, 2004)

110. Programme MAB. *Biosphere Reserve Information. Kenya. Malindi-Watamu.* http://www2.unesco.org/mab/br/brdir/directory/biores.asp?code=KEN+03&mode=all (Accessed December 26, 2004)

111. ICRAN. *Malindi and Watamu Marine National Park and Reserve.* www.icran.org (Accessed December 26, 2003)

112. Kaunda-Arara B and GA Rose 2004. Effects of marine reef National Parks on fishery CPUE in coastal Kenya. *Biological Conservation*, **118**: 1-13

113. Muthiga N, S Riedmiller, R van der Elst, J mann-Lan, C Horrill, and T McClanahan 2000. Management, In: *Coral Reefs of the Indian Ocean: Their Ecology and Conservation*, by T McClanahan, C Sheppard, and D Obura (eds). Oxford University Press: New York, USA. pp 473-505

114. Muthiga N, S Weru, J Kareko, and B Musyoki 2002. *The management status of Malindi-Watamu marine protected area complex.* FAO; UNEP; KWS; ICRAN.

115. McClanahan T, N Muthiga, and B Kaunda-Arara 2001. *The biophysical and ecological profile of the Malindi Watamu marine protected area complex.* UNEP; ICRAN; KWS.

116. ICRAN. *Dar es Salaam Marine Reserve (DMRS).* http://www.icran.org/SITES/doc/dmrs.pdf (Accessed January 10, 2004)

117. Wagner GM, U Mallya, S Juma, Y Mgaya, O Wahure, G Mahika, and S Wagner 1999. *A preliminary investigation for an integrated, community – based approach to conservation and restoration of marine ecosystems along the Dar es Salaam Coast.* African Foundation: Dar es Salaam.

118. Anonymous. *Dar es Salaam Marine Reserve System Socio-economic Assessment.* pp 57-71

119. Kamukuru A 1998. *Assessment of biological status of the Dar es Salaam Marine reserves off the Tanzanian Coast.* In Proceedings of the first WIOMSA Scientific Symposium. WIOMSA

120. Mohammed SM, C Muhando, and H Machano 2002. Assessment of Coral Reef Degradation in Tanzania; Results of Coral Reef Monitoring 1999 -2002, In: *Coral Reef Degradation in the Indian Ocean*, by O Linden, D Sauter, D Wilhelmsson, and D Obura (eds)

121. Rodgers WA , LB Mwasumbi, and JB Hall 1985. *The floristic of the three coastal forests near Dar es Salaam.* Department of Zoology & Botany of the University of Dar es Salaam; The Division of Forestry, Sokoine University of Agriculture, Morogoro Tanzania.

122. Ming Chou L, V Si Tuan, P Reefs, T Yeemin, A Cabanban, S Kessna, and I Kessna 2002. Status of Southeast Asia coral reefs, In: *Status of Coral Reefs of the World: 2002*, by C Wilkinson (ed). Australian Institute of Marine Science: Townsville, Australia. pp 123-142

123. UNEP. *About East Asian Seas Action Plan.* http://www.unep.org/unep/regoffs/roap/easrcu/about_eas.htm (Accessed May 20, 2004)

124. ICRAN. *Gili Matra Marine Natural Recreation Park West Nusa Tenggara Province – Indonesia.* http://www.icran.org/SITES/doc/WS_gili.pdf (Accessed January 2, 2004)

125. ICRAN 2002. Bunaken National Park, Indonesia – ICRAN demonstration site, In: *Status of Corals Reefs of the World: 2002*, by C Wilkinson (ed). Australian Institute of Marine Science: Townsville, Australia. p 144

126. NOAA. *Bunaken national Park, Indonesia.* http://effectivempa.noaa.gov/sites/bunaken.html (Accessed January 2, 2004)

127. Erdmann MV and PR Merrill. *Multiple-use Zoning in Marine Protected Areas: Bunaken National Park a case study.* USAID, Indonesia. pp 5

128. Anonymous. *Bunaken Entrance Fee FAQ Sheet.* http://www.bunaken.or.id/DownLoad/Bunaken%20Entrance%20Fee%20FAQ%20Sheet%20English.pdf (Accessed January 20, 2004)

129. Anonymous 2003. *British Airways Honors Bunaken National marine Park for 'Tourism of Tomorrow' Award.* http://www.bunaken.info/nswa_news.html#award (Accessed January 30, 2004)

130. Erdman MV 2003. *Bunaken National Park entrance fee system struggling in the wake of global tourism downturn.* http://www.bunaken.info/nrm_news16.html#3 (Accessed January 30, 2004)

131. WWF. *Marine ecosystems of the South Pacific are among the most important natural assets on Earth.* http://www.wwfpacific.org.fj/marineecoindex.htm (Accessed January 10, 2004)

132. Anonymous. *People and resources in the Pacific Islands – An overview.* http://www.toryread.com/projimg/ppdfs/stories2.pdf (Accessed January 28, 2004)

133. Sulu R, R Cumming, L Wantiez, L Kumar, A Mulipola, M Lober, S Sauni, T Poulasi, and K Pakoa 2002. Status of coral reefs in the southwest Pacific to 2002: Fiji, Nauru, New Caledonia, Samoa, Solomon Islands, Tuvalu and Vanuatu, In: *Status of Coral Reefs of the World: 2002*, by C Wilkinson (ed). Australian Institute of Marine Science: Townsville, Australia. pp 181-213

134. Power M 2004. personal communication

135. Maragos J 1998. Status of coral reefs of the southwest and east Pacific: Melanesia and Polynesia, In: *Status of Coral reefs of the World: 1998*, by C Wilkinson (ed). Australian Institute of Marine Science: Townsville, Australia

136. Salvat B 2002. Status of Southeast and Central Pacific coral reefs 'Polynesia Mana Node': Cook Islands, French polynesia, Kiribati, Niue, Tokelau, Tonga, Wallis and Futuna, In: *Status of Coral Reefs of the World: 2002*, by C Wilkinson (ed). Australian Institute of Marine Science: Townsville, Australia. pp 203-213

137. Goreau T 2002. *Global warming kills South Pacific coral reefs.* http://globalcoral.org/GLOBAL%20WARMING%20KILLS%20SOUTH%20PACIFIC%20CORAL%20REEFS.htm (Accessed January 29, 2004)

138. ICRAN. *The South Pacific.* http://coral.unep.ch/icranpls.htm (Accessed January 15, 2004)

139. SPREP. *SPREP's structure.* http://www.sidsnet.org/pacific/sprep/sprep/about.htm (Accessed January 19, 2004)

140. SPREP. *What's SPREP.* http://www.sidsnet.org/pacific/sprep/whatsprep_.htm (Accessed January 25, 2004)

141. UNDP. *UNDP and Capacity 21.* http://www.undp.org/capacity21/ (Accessed June 3, 2004)

142. ICRAN 2002. Jaluit Atoll Marine Conservation Area, Marshall Islands – ICRAN Demonstration Site, In: *Status of Coral Reefs of the World: 2002*, by C Wilkinson (ed). Australian Institute of Marine Science: Townsville, Australia. p 236

143. Lindsay S 2002. Marine Resource Survey and Assessment of Jaluit Atoll, Republic of the Marshall Islands. *SPC Fisheries Newsletter*, **103**: 13-16

144. Anonymous. *Jaluit MPA to receive new funding through ICRAN.* (Accessed January 19, 2004)

145. NFWF 2002. *Coral Reef Conservation Projects Funded in 2002.* http://www.nfwf.org/programs/coral2002.htm (Accessed January 29, 2004)

146. RAMSAR 2003. *Wetlands International announces DGIS small grant awards for 2003.* (Accessed January 29, 2004)

147. ICRAN 2003. *ICRAN Progress and activities, April 2003.* (Accessed January 30, 2004)

148. ICRAN. *ICRAN in Jaluit Atoll.* pp 2

149. Wilkinson C 1998. *Status of coral reefs of the world: 1998.* Global Coral Reef Monitoring Network; Australian Institute of Marine Science: Townsville, Australia. pp 184

150. Nzali LM, RW Johnstone, and YD Mgaya 1998. Factors affecting scleractinian coral recruitment on a nearshore reef in Tanzania. *Ambio*, **27**(8): 717-722

151. McManus JW 1997. *Tropical marine fisheries and the future of coral reefs: A brief review with emphasis on Southeast Asia.* In Proceedings of the 8th International Coral Reef Symposium. Vol. 1. pp 129-134

152. Edward A 1999. *Coral reef and coastal resource use in Micronesia.* In Proceedings of the International Conference on Scientific Aspects of Coral Reef Assessment, Monitoring and Restoration, NCRI. Fort Lauderdale, USA. p 83

153. Rogers CS, L McLain, and E Zullo 1988. *Damage to coral reefs in Virgin Islands National Park and Biosphere Reserve from recreational activities.* In Proceedings of the 6th International Coral Reef Symposium. Vol. 2. pp 405-410

154. Maragos JE 1974. *Coral transplantation: a method to create, preserve and manage coral reefs*. Sea Grant Advisory Report, Number UNIH-SEAGRANT-AR-74-03, Cormar-14. pp 30

155. Clark S and AJ Edwards 1995. Coral transplantation as an aid to reef rehabilitation: evaluation of a case study in the Maldive Islands. *Coral Reefs*, **14**: 201-213

156. Brown BE and RP Dunne 1988. The environmental impact of coral mining on coral reefs in the Maldives. *Environmental Conservation*, **15**: 159-166

157. Berg H, MC Ohman, S Troeng, and O Linden 1998. Environmental economics of coral reef destruction in Sri Lanka. *Ambio*, **27**(8): 627-634

158. Dulvy NK, D Stanwell-Smith, WRT Darwall, and CJ Horrill 1995. Coral mining at Mafia Island, Tanzania: a management dilemna. *Ambio*, **24**: 358-365

159. Franklin H, CA Muhando, and U Lindahl 1998. Coral culturing and temporal recruitment patterns in Zanzibar, Tanzania. *Ambio*, **27**(8): 651-655

160. Green E and F Shirley 1999. *The global trade in coral*. UNEP World Conservation Monitoring Centre: Cambridge, UK. WCMC Biodiversity Series, Number 9. pp 70

161. Oliver J and P McGinnity 1985. *Commercial coral collecting on the Great Barrier Reef*. In Proceedings of the 5th International Coral Reef Symposium. Vol. 5. pp 563-568

162. Riegl B and KE Luke 1998. Ecological parameters of dynamited reefs in the northern Red Sea and their relevance to reef rehabilitation. *Marine Pollution Bulletin*, **37**(8-12): 488-498

163. Lindahl U 1998. Low-tech restoration of degraded coral reefs through transplantation of staghorn corals. *Ambio*, **37**(8): 645-650

164. Fox HE, RL Caldwell, and JS Pet 1999. *Enhancing coral reef recovery after destructive fishing practices in Indonesia*. In Proceedings of the International Conference on Scientific Aspects of Coral reef Assessment, Monitoring and Restoration, NCRI. Fort Lauderdale, USA. p 88

165. Bowden-Kerby A 1997. *Coral transplantation in sheltered habitats using unattached fragments and cultured colonies*. In Proceedings of the 8th International Coral Reef Symposium. Vol. 2. pp 2063-2068

166. Bowden-Kerby A 2001. Low-tech coral reef restoration methods modelled after natural fragmentation processes. *Bulletin of Marine Science*, **69**(2): 915-931

167. Jackson BC 1997. *Reefs since Colombus*. In Proceedings of the 8th International Coral Reef Symposium. Vol. 1. pp 97-106

168. Hughes TP 1989. Community structure and diversity of coral reefs: The role of history. *Ecology*, **70**: 275-279

169. Hughes TP 1994. Catastrophes, phase shifts and large scale degradation of a Caribbean coral reef. *Science*, **265**: 1547-1551

170. Done TJ 1992. Phase shifts in coral reef communities and their ecological significance. *Hydrobiologia*, **247**: 121-132

171. Szmant AM 1997. *Nutrient effects on coral reefs: A hypothesis on the importance of topographic and trophic complexity to reef nutrient dynamics*. In Proceedings of the 8th International Coral Reef Symposium. Vol. 2. pp 1527-1532

172. Grigg RW and JE Marigos 1974. Recolonization of hermatypic corals on submerged lava flows in Hawaii. *Ecology*, **55**: 387-395

173. Stoddart DR 1974. *Post hurricane changes on the British Honduras reefs: resurvey of 1972*. In Proceedings of the 2nd International Coral Reef Symposium. Vol. 2. pp 473-483

174. Pearson RG 1981. Recovery and colonization of coral reefs. *Marine Ecology Progress Series*, **4**: 105-122

175. Endean R 1973. Population explosions of *Acanthaster plancii* and associated destruction of hermatypic corals in the Indo-West Pacific region, In: *Biology and geology of coral reefs*, by O Jones and R Endean (eds). Academic Press: New York, USA. pp 389-438

176. Highsmith RC, AC Riggs, and CM d'Antonio 1980. Survival of hurricane generated coral fragments and a disturbance model of reef calcification/growth rates. *Oecologia*, **46**: 322-329

177. Shinn E 1976. Coral reef recovery in Florida and the Persian Gulf. *Environmental Geology*, **1**: 241-254

178. Connell JH 1973. Population ecology of reef building corals, In: *Biology and geology of coral reefs*, by O Jones and R Endean (eds). Academic Press: New York, USA. pp 205-245

179. Harrison PJ and CC Wallace 1990. Reproduction, dispersal and recruitment of scleractinian corals, In: *Ecosystems of the World: Coral Reefs*, by Z Dubinsky (ed). Elsevier Science Publisher: Amsterdam, Holland. pp 133-208

180. Highsmith RC 1982. Reproduction by fragmentation in corals. *Marine Ecology Progress Series*, **7**: 207-226

181. Birkeland CE 1988. Second order ecological effects of nutrient input into coral communities. *Galaxea*, **7**: 91-100

182. Wittenberg M and W Hunte 1992. Effects of eutrophication and sedimentation on juvenile corals. *Marine Biology*, **112**: 131-138

183. Gleason MG 1999. *The importance of algal-grazer interactions in early growth and survivorship of sexual recruits and transplanted juvenile corals.* In Proceedings of the International Conference on Scientific Aspects of Coral Reef Assessment, Monitoring and Restoration, NCRI. Fort Lauderdale. p 93

184. Hodgson G 1990. Sediment and the settlement of the reef coral *Pocillopora damicornis. Coral Reefs*, **9**: 41-43

185. Maida M, JC Coll, and PW Sammarco 1994. Shedding new light on coral recruitment. *Journal of Experimental Marine Biology and Ecology*, **180**: 189-202

186. Babcock R and C Mundy 1996. Coral recruitment: Consequences of settlement choice for early growth and survivorship in two scleractinians. *Journal of Experimental Marine Biology and Ecology*, **206**: 179-201

187. Quinn NJ and BL Kojis 1999. *Case studies of natural variability in coral recruitment from the Caribbean and Pacific. Which reefs need restoration assistance.* In Proceedings of the International Conference on Scientific Aspects of Coral Reef Assessment, Monitoring and Restoration, NCRI. Fort Lauderdale, USA. p 159

188. Sousa WP 1984. The role of disturbance in natural communities. *Annual Review of Ecology and Systematics*, **15**: 353-391

189. Bothwell AM 1981. *Fragmentation, a means of asexual reproduction and dispersal in the coral genus Acropora (Scleractinia: astrocoeniida) – a preliminary report.* In Proceedings of the 4th International Coral Reef Symposium. Vol. 2. pp 137-144

190. Tunnicliffe V 1981. Breakage and propagation of the stony coral *Acropora cervicornis. Proceedings of the National Academy of Sciences of the United States*, **78**: 2427-2431

191. Gilmore MD and BR Hall 1976. Life history, growth habits and constructional roles of *Acropora cervicornis* in patch reef environment. *Journal of Sedimentary Petrology*, **46**: 519-522

192. Harriott VJ and DA Fisk 1988. *Coral transplantation as a reef management option.* In Proceedings of the 6th International Coral Reef Symposium. Vol. 2. pp 375-379

193. Hatcher BG, RE Johannes, and AI Robertson 1989. Review of research relevant to the conservation of shallow tropical marine systems. *Oceanography and marine Biology. An Annual Review*, **27**: 334-414

194. Maragos JE 1992. Restoring coral reefs with emphasis on Pacific reefs, In: *Restoring the nation's marine environment*, by G Thayer (ed). Maryland Seagrant: College Park, USA. pp 141-122

195. Edwards AJ and S Clark 1998. Coral transplantation: a useful management tool or misguided meddling? *Marine Pollution Bulletin*, **37**: 474-487

196. Birkeland CE 1999. *Is management of reefs a rational approach?* In Proceedings of the International Conference on Scientific Aspects of Coral Reef Assessment, Monitoring and Restoration, NCRI. Fort Lauderdale, USA. p 55

197. Challenger GE 1999. *Questions regarding the biological significance of vessel groundings and appropriateness of restoration effort.* In Proceedings of the International Conference on Scientific Aspects of Coral Reef Assessment, Monitoring and Restoration, NCRI. Fort Lauderdale. p 66

198. Guzman HM 1991. Restoration of coral reefs in Pacific Costa Rica. *Conservation Biology*, **5**(2): 189-195

199. Guzman HM 1993. *Restoration of eastern Pacific coral reefs (Costa Rica, Panama and Colombia): an approach to monitor regional biodiversity.* WWF-Biodiversity Support Program. Final Report.

200. Bowden-Kerby A 2001. *Coral transplantation modeled after natural fragmentation processes: Low-tech tools for coral reef restoration and management.* University of Puerto Rico at Mayaguez. pp. 195

201. Harriott VJ and DA Fisk 1988. *Accelerated regeneration of hard corals: a manual for coral reef users and managers.* GBRMPA Technical Memorandum, Number 16. pp 39

202. Bell JD and R Galzin 1984. Influence of live coral cover on coral reef fish communities. *Marine Ecology Progress Series*, **15**: 265-274

203. Bell JD, ML Harmelin-Vivien, and R Galzin 1985. *Large scale spatial variation in abundance of butterflyfishes (Chaetondontidae) on polynesian reefs*. In Proceedings of the 5th International Coral Reef Symposium. Vol. 5. pp 421-426

204. Jones GP 1988. Experimental evaluation of the effects of habitat structure and competitive interaction in the juveniles of two coral reef fishes. *Journal of Experimental Marine Biology and Ecology*, **123**: 115-126

205. Sale PF 1991. *The Ecology of Fishes on Coral Reefs*. Academic Press: San Diego, USA. pp 754

206. Brock RE 1979. An experimental study on the effects of grazing by parrotfishes and role of refuges in benthic community structure. *Marine Biology*, **51**: 381-388

207. McClanahan TR, V Hendricks, and NVC Polunin 1999. *Varying response of herbivorous and invertebrate feeding fishes to macroalgal reduction: a restoration experiment*. In Proceedings of the International Conference on Scientific Aspects of Coral Reef Assessment, Monitoring and Restoration, NCRI. Fort Lauderdale, USA. p 133

208. World Bank 1999. *Voices from the village: A comparative study of coastal resource management in the Pacific Islands.* World Bank Papua New Guinea and Pacific Island Country Management Unit. Pacific Islands Discussion Paper Series, Number 9. pp 99

209. Connell JH 1997. Disturbance and recovery of coral assemblages. *Coral Reefs Supplement*, **16**(S): 101-113

210. Glynn PW and JL Mate 1997. *Field guide to the Pacific coral reefs of Panama*. In Proceedings of the 8th International Coral Reef Symposium. Vol. 1. pp 145-166

211. Ortiz-Prosper AL and WA Bowden-Kerby 1999. *Transformation of artificial concrete "reef ball" structure into living coral heads through the use of implants of juvenile massive corals*. In Proceedings of the International Conference on Scientific Aspects of Coral Reef Assessment, Monitoring and Restoration, NCRI. Fort Lauderdale, USA. p 148

ACRONYMS

AGRRA	Atlantic and Gulf Rapid Reef Assessment
AMEP	Assessment and Management of Environmental Pollution
ASSETS	Arabuko-Sokoke Schools & Eco-Tourism Scheme
AusAID	Australian Agency for International Development
BNP	Bunaken National Park
BRMP	Buccoo Reef Marine Park
CANARI	Caribbean Natural Resources Institute
CAR/RCU	Caribbean Regional Co-ordinating Unit (see also UNEP CAR/RCU)
CARICOMP	Caribbean Coastal Marine Productivity Programme
CASO	Conservation Area Supporting Officer
CBD	Convention on Biological Diversity
CC:TRAIN	Climate Change Training programme
C-CAM	Caribbean Coastal Area Management Foundation
CCDC	Caribbean Coastal Data Centre
CEP	Caribbean Environment Programme (see also UNEP CEP)
CI	Conservation International
COBSEA	Coordinating Body on the Seas of East Asia
COCATRAM	Comisión Centroamericana de Transporte Marítimo (Central American Commission for Maritime Transport)
CONANP	Comisión Nacional de Areas Naturales Protegidas (National Comission for Natural Protected Areas)
CORAL	Coral Reef Alliance
CORDIO	Coral Reef Degradation in the Indian Ocean
COREMAP	Coral Reef Rehabilitation and Management Programme
COT	Crown of Thorns starfish
CPPS	Comisión Permanente del Pacifico Sur (Permanent Comission of the South Pacific)
CRCP	Coral Reef Conservation Project
CZMC	Coastal Zone Management Centre
DFID	Department for International Development
DMRS	Dar es Salaam Marine Reserves System
DOF	Department of Fisheries
DPTNB	Bunaken National Park Management Advisory Board
EAF/RCU	Eastern African Regional Coordinating Unit (see also UNEP EAF/RCU)
EAS/RCU	East Asian Seas Regional Coordinating Unit (see also UNEP EAS/RCU)
EC	European Commission
EIA	Environmental Impact Assessment
EPIQ	Environmental Policy and Institutional Strengthening
ERFEN	Estudio Regional del Fenómeno El Niño
EU	European Union
FAD	Fish Aggregating Device
FAO	Food and Agriculture Organization of the United Nations
FPA	Fishing Priority Area
FSPI	Foundation for the Peoples of the South Pacific International
GCRMN	Global Coral Reef Monitoring Network
GEF	Global Environment Facility
GEMPA	Group of Experts in MPA
GIWA	Global International Water Assessment
GM-MNRP	Gili Matra Marine Natural Recreation Park
GMP	General Management Plan
GOSL	Government of Saint Lucia
GPA	Global Plan of Action for the Protection of the Marine Environment from Land Based Sources of Pollution
HAB	Harmful Algal Blooms
HELCOM	The Helsinki Commission
ICAM	Integrated Coastal Area Management
ICLARM	The International Center for Living Aquatic Resources Management now renamed The WorldFish Centre
ICM	Integrated Coastal Management
ICRAN	International Coral Reef Action Network
ICRI	International Coral Reef Initiative
ICRI-CPC	International Coral Reef Initiative-Coordination and Planning Committee
ICRIN	International Coral Reef Information Network
ICZM	Integrated Coastal Zone Managament
IMA	Institute of Marine Affairs
IMO	International Maritime Organization
IOC UNESCO	Intergovernmental Oceanographic Commission of the United Nations Educational, Scientific and Cultural Organization
ITMEMS	International Tropical Marine Ecosystems Management Symposium
IUCN	The World Conservation Union

IUCN-EARO	IUCN Regional Office for East Africa	SPBCP	South Pacific Biodiversity Conservation Programme
JACA	Jaluit Atoll Conservation Area	SPREP	South Pacific Regional Environment Programme
JCRMN	Jamaican Coral Reef Monitoring Network	SRDF	Soufriere Regional Development Foundation
KMFRI	Kenya Marine and Fisheries Research Institute	STINAPA	Stichting Nationale Parken Bonaire
KWS	Kenya Wildlife Service	TAC	Technical Advisory Committee
LBS	Protocol on Land Based Sources of Marine Pollution	TCMP	Tanzania Coastal Management Partnership
MAB	Man and the Biosphere	THA	Tobago House of Assembly
MAC	Marine Aquarium Council	TNC	The Nature Conservancy
MBRS	Mesoamerican Barrier Reef System	UN	United Nations
MEA	Multilateral Environmental Agreements	UNCED	United Nations Conference on Environment and Development
MPA	Marine Protected Area	UNDP	United Nations Development Programme
MR	Marine Reserve	UNDP SGP	UNDP Small Grants Programme
NEMS	National Environment Management Strategies	UNEP	United Nations Environment Programme
NFWF	National Fish and Wildlife Foundation	UNEP-CAR/RCU	United Nations Environment Programme – Caribbean Regional Coordinating Unit
NGO	Non-Governmental Organization		
NOAA	National Oceanic and Atmospheric Administration	UNEP CEP	United Nations Environment Programme Caribbean Environment Programme
NOWPAP	Northwest Pacific Action Plan	UNEP EAF/RCU	United Nations Environment Programme – East African Regional Coordinating Unit
NRM	National Resource Management		
OCA/PAC	Oceans and Coastal Areas Programme Activity Centre of UNEP	UNEP EAS/RCU	United Nations Environment Programme – East Asian Seas Regional Coordinating Unit
OCPC	Office of the Chief Parliamentary Counsel	UNEP IUC	United Nations Environment Programme Information Unit on Conventions
OSPAR	Oslo and Paris Commission	UNEP – WCMC	United Nations Environment Programme World Conservation Monitoring Centre
PBFMC	Portland Bight Fisheries Management Council		
PBPA	The Portland Bight Protected Area	UNESO	United Nations Educational, Scientific and Cultural Organization
PICCAP	Pacific Island Climate Change Assistance Programme	UNF	United Nations Foundation
PROPEPA	Procuraduría Federal de Protección al Ambiente	UNFCCC	United Nations Framework Convention on Climate Change
RAMSAR	Convention on Wetlands signed in Ramsar (Iran)	UNITAR	United Nations Institute for Training and Research
RAP	Regional Action Plan	USAID	United States Agency for International Development
RBBCH	Banco Chincorro Biosphere Reserve		
RMIEPA	Republic of the Marshall Islands Environmental Protection Authority	USP	University of the South Pacific
		WCPA	World Commission on Protected Areas
ROPME	Regional Organization for the Protection of the Marine Environment	WCS	Wildlife Conservation Society
		WEHAB	Water, Energy, Health, Agriculture and Biodiversity
SACEP	South Asia Co-operative Environment Programme	WIOMSA	Western Indian Ocean Marine Science Association
SAGARPA	Secretaría de Agricultura, Ganadería, Desarollo Rural, Pesca y Alimentación	WorldFish Centre	See ICLARM
		WRI	World Resources Institute
SIDA	Swedish Development Agency	WSSD	World Summit on Sustainable Development
SMMA	Soufriere Marine Management Area	WWF	World Wildlife Fund
SPAW	Protocol on Specially Protected Areas and Wildlife		

CONTACTS

Training of Trainers, Caribbean:
Malden Miller
ICRAN Caribbean Coordinator
United Nations Environment Programme
Caribbean Environment Programme
14-20 Port Royal Street
Kingston, Jamaica
E-mail: mwm.uneprcuja@cwjamaica.com

Sian Ka'an Biosphere Reserve:
Oscar Alvarez
Coordinator
ICRAN-MAR Project
Coastal Resources Multicomplex Building,
Fisheries Departament,
Princess Margaret Drive,
Belize City, Belize.
E-mail: oalvarez@icran.org,
siankaan@prodigy.net.mx

Banco Chinchorro:
Tomás Camarena Luhrs
Dirección de la Reserva de la Biosfera Banco
Chinchorro
Blvd. Kukulcán Km 4.8 Zona Hotelera
C.P. 77500 Cancún,
Quintana Roo
Mexico
E-mail chinchorro@conanp.gob.mx
bchinchorro@prodigy.net.mx

Bonaire National Marine Park:
Ramón de León
Manager
PO Box 368, Kralendijk
Bonaire, Netherlands Antilles
Dutch Caribbean
Email: marinepark@stinapa.org

Soufriere Marine Management Area:
Dawn Pierre-Nathoniel
Fisheries Biologist
Department of Fisheries
Ministry of Agriculture, Forestry and Fisheries
Pointe Seraphine
CASTRIES
St Lucia
E-mail: deptfish@slumaffe.org ;
dawnpierrenathoniel@hotmail.com

Portland Bight Protected Area:
Peter Espeut
Executive Director
Caribbean Coastal Area Management
Foundation
P.O. Box 33, Lionel Town,
Clarendon, JAMAICA
Email: pespeut@infochan.com

Pigeon Point, Tobago:
Arthur C. Potts
Director Marine Resources and Fisheries,
Department of Marine Resources and Fisheries,
Division of Agriculture, Marine Affairs and
Environment, Tobago House of Assembly,
TLH Building, Scarborough,
c/o P.O. Box 516 Scarborough PO,
Tobago
Republic of Trinidad and Tobago
E-mail: acpotts@tstt.net.tt , artpotts@hotmail.com

Malindi-Watamu Marine Park Reserves:
Dr. Nyawira Muthiga
Senior Marine Scientist
Wildlife Conservation Society
P.O. Box 82144
Mombasa
Kenya
E-mail: nmuthiga@africaonline.co.ke

Dar es Salaam Marine Reserves System:
Chikambi Rumisha
Marine Parks and Reserves HQ
Olympio Street, Plot 951
P. O. Box 7565
Dar es Salaam
Email: ckrumisha@hotmail.com

Gili Matra Marine Park:
Edi Djuharsa
Gili Matra Marine Park
Natural Resources Conservation Office
West Nusa Tenggara
Indonesia
E-mail: edidj@post.com

Bunaken National Marine Park:
Maxi Wowiling
Program Manager
Bunaken National Park Management
Advisory Board (DPTNB)
Bunaken National Marine Park,
Bunaken Island,
North Sulawesi,
Indonesia
E-mail: dptnb@indosat.net.id

Jaluit Atoll Marine Conservation Area:
Mr John Bungitak
Director
Environmental Protection Authority
Majuro
Marshall Islands
E-mail: rmiepa@ntamar.com, eparmi@ntamar.com

Coral Transplantation and Restocking
Austin Bowden Kerby, PhD
Program Scientist, Coral Gardens Initiative
Foundation of the Peoples of the South Pacific
Counterpart International
Suva, Fiji Islands
E-mail: austin.bowdenkerby@fspi.org.fj

DATE DUE

MAR 2 1 2011			
APR 1 1 2011			

DEMCO 138298

E.05.III.D.12

www.unep.org
United Nations Environment Programme
P.O. Box 30552, Nairobi, Kenya
Tel: 254 20 621234
Fax: 254 20 623927
Email: cpiinfo@unep.org
web:www.unep.org

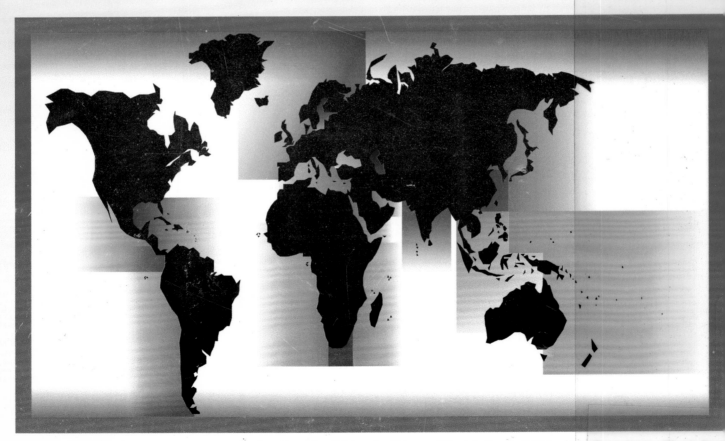

**West to East: North-East Pacific South-East Pacific Wider Caribbean West & Central Africa Mediterranean Black Sea
Eastern Africa   Red Sea & Gulf of Aden   ROPME Sea Area   South Asian Seas   East Asian Seas   North-West Pacific
South Pacific Partner programmes: Arctic North-East Atlantic Baltic Sea Caspian Sea Antarctic**

INTERNATIONAL MONETARY AND FINANCIAL ISSUES FOR THE 1990s

Volume VIII

UNITED NATIONS